The Naval & Military Press Ltd

A SHORT HISTORY
OF
30 CORPS
IN THE EUROPEAN CAMPAIGN.
1944 — 1945.

Published by

The Naval & Military Press Ltd
Unit 5 Riverside, Brambleside
Bellbrook Industrial Estate
Uckfield, East Sussex
TN22 1QQ England

Tel: +44 (0)1825 749494

www.naval-military-press.com
www.nmarchive.com

Back cover image: Lieutenant-General Horrocks addresses XXX Corps staff at Rees on the banks of the Rhine, 26 May 1945.

In reprinting in facsimile from the original, any imperfections are inevitably reproduced and the quality may fall short of modern type and cartographic standards.

CONTENTS

	Page
30 Corps	5
Foreword	7

Chapter I. The Assault on the Beaches and the Advance to the Seine   9
    a) Operation Overlord: The Plan 9
    b) Establishment of the Beachhead 10
    c) The Development of the Beachhead 14
    d) The Breakthrough to the Seine 18

Chapter II. The Capture of Antwerp 23
    a) The Seine and the Somme 23
    b) The Advance to Antwerp and Brussels 25
    c) Crossing the Canals 27

Chapter III. The Advance to Arnhem 31
    a) From the Escaut to the Waal 31
    b) The Crossing of the Waal 33
    c) The Fighting on "The Island" 35
    d) The Withdrawal from Arnhem 37

Chapter IV. The Roer Valley 41
    12. November — 13. December 1944 41

Chapter V. The Battle of the Ardennes 47
    a) The German Offensive 47
    b) The Defence of Brussels 48
    c) The Defence of the Meuse 49
    d) The German Withdrawal 51

	Page
Chapter VI. The Reichswald Battle	55
a) Operation Veritable	55
b) The Plan	57
c) The Assault	59
d) The Advance towards Goch	62
e) The Attack on Goch	64
f) The Battles for Weeze	65
g) The Advance to Wesel	66
Chapter VII. Across the Rhine and into Germany	69
a) The Crossing of the Rhine	69
b) The Breakout from the Bridge-head	72
c) The Approach to Bremen	74
d) The Capture of Bremen	75
e) The Last Battles	76

Appendices

A	Operation Overlord: Order of Battle	79
B	Operation Market Garden: Order of Battle	81
C	Operation Veritable: Order of Battle	83
D	Operation Veritable: Outline Artillery Fire Plan	85
E	Operation Plunder: Order of Battle	87
F	Itinerary of Main Corps HQ	89

30 Corps

For 30 Corps, the journey to victory began at Alamein, in Africa; it was to end near Bremen, in Germany. It was not a direct road, nor was it short. But always it led forward and throughout its course there was no turning back.

The first stage in the journey took the Corps across the deserts to success at Tunis. Then came its first sea voyage, across the narrows of the Mediterranean, to victory in Sicily.

It was from Sicily in October 1943, that it received its summons to England. Before Christmas that year, Corps HQ with 50 (Northumbrian) and 51 (Highland) Divisions, 8 Armoured Brigade and 5 AGRA, had reached home, and were followed in January by 7 Armoured Div from Italy.

It soon became known that the Corps had been selected to take its part, as an assaulting formation, in the forthcoming invasion of Europe. Towards the end of January 1944, Advanced Corps HQ moved to London to start planning its share in Operation Overlord, as the great seaborne operation was called. Throughout the Spring days of 1944, planning and preparations, strengthened by the experiences in Sicily, went on. In April, concentration of the Corps Troops commenced and by the end of May, the Corps and its Divisions were arrayed around the coasts of Britain from Harwich to Southampton.

Soon the signs of "Club route", which had crossed the deserts of Africa and the isle of Sicily, would be pointing the way through France. Within nine months they would cross a British bridge over the Rhine; within the year, they would lead the Corps to its final victory in Germany.

FOREWORD

This book gives an outline of the operations of 30 Corps in France, Belgium, Holland and Germany during 1944—1945.

It is as accurate as possible and will, I hope, serve as a background for officers who wish to tell their troops about the battle; it may also be a reminder to members of the Corps of the battles which they helped to win and be a framework on which future authors can build full and attractive stories.

Nienburg,
Hanover
July 1945

B. G. Horrocks
Lt Gen.
Commander 30 Corps.

CHAPTER ONE

The Assault on the Beaches
and
the Advance to the Seine

Operation Overlord — The Plan

The assault forces of 21 Army Group to be employed in the opening stages of operation Overland consisted of the First US Army, with V and VII US Corps, and the Second British Army with 1 and 30 Corps. They were associated with the Allied Naval Expeditionary Force and the Allied Expeditionary Air Force.

The commander in Chief, General B. L. Montgomery, intended to assault simultaneously north of the Carentan estuary and between the Carentan estuary and the river Orne with the object of securing a lodgement area, including the port of Cherbourg, as a base for further operations. First US Army was to land on the right of Second Army and was given the initial task of capturing the Cotentin peninsula including in particular the port of Cherbourg, and subsequently of securing Angers, Nantes and the Brittany ports.

Second Army's task was to protect the left flank of First US Army. The Army Commander, Lt. General M. Dempsey planned, by assaulting between Port en Bessin and the river Orne, to secure and develop a bridgehead south of the line St Lo—Caen and to obtain possession of the airfield sites southeast of Caen.

Over six thousand aircraft of the AEAF and large naval forces would be available to support the assaulting troops.

The Second Army assault was to be carried out on a two Corps front — 30 Corps * right, 1 Corps left. The Army plan was divided into four phases which are shown on Map 2. Airborne landings were

---

* 30 Corps Order of Battle, Appendix "A"

to be made on both flanks of the Army Group front during the night D—1/D Day and the seaborne forces were to assault early on D Day.

The 30 Corps Commander's plan for D Day was to assault the localities Le Hamel and La Rivière with the co-operation of Naval Assault Force G and then to secure the high ground due south of the beaches and southeast of Bayeux. Exploitation to the area Villers Bocage, as a pivot for subsequent manoeuvre, was also ordered to take place on D Day. 47 (RM) Commando, under command 30 Corps, was to capture Port en Bessin and the coast defence battery at Longues.

50 (N) Div, with 69 and 231 Inf Brigades leading, supported by DD tanks of 8th Armd Bde, was to carry out the assault. Following up, 7 Armd Div and 49 Div would start disembarking about last light on D Day and D + 4 respectively.

The target date (known as Y Day), by which all preparations had to be completed, was fixed for 1 June 1944. The day of the operation, D Day, would be notified later.

Establishment of the Beachead (Map 3)

After an initial postponement of one day, D Day was ordered to be 6 June 1944. H hour was fixed at 0725 hrs (BDST) and was described as the time at which the leading assault craft touched the beaches. During the night 5/6 June, a heavy bombing attack was directed against all known enemy coastal defences and then, in the moonlight early on 6 June, the airborne forces landed.

As the landing craft got under weigh in the darkness on 5 June, the weather did not look propitious for a seaborne assault. There was a heavy swell running and a strong wind was blowing down the Channel. The worst fears of those prone to sickness were realised as the craft got out into the open sea and many troops were sick, wet and cold, before they landed. V US Corps, on the right flank of 30 Corps, met particularly unfavourable conditions on their beaches, where high seas were running. Many landing craft capsized and few of their amphibious tanks reached the beaches. Except for some difficulties with craft "broaching to", the 30 Corps landings proceeded satisfactorily.

MAP 1

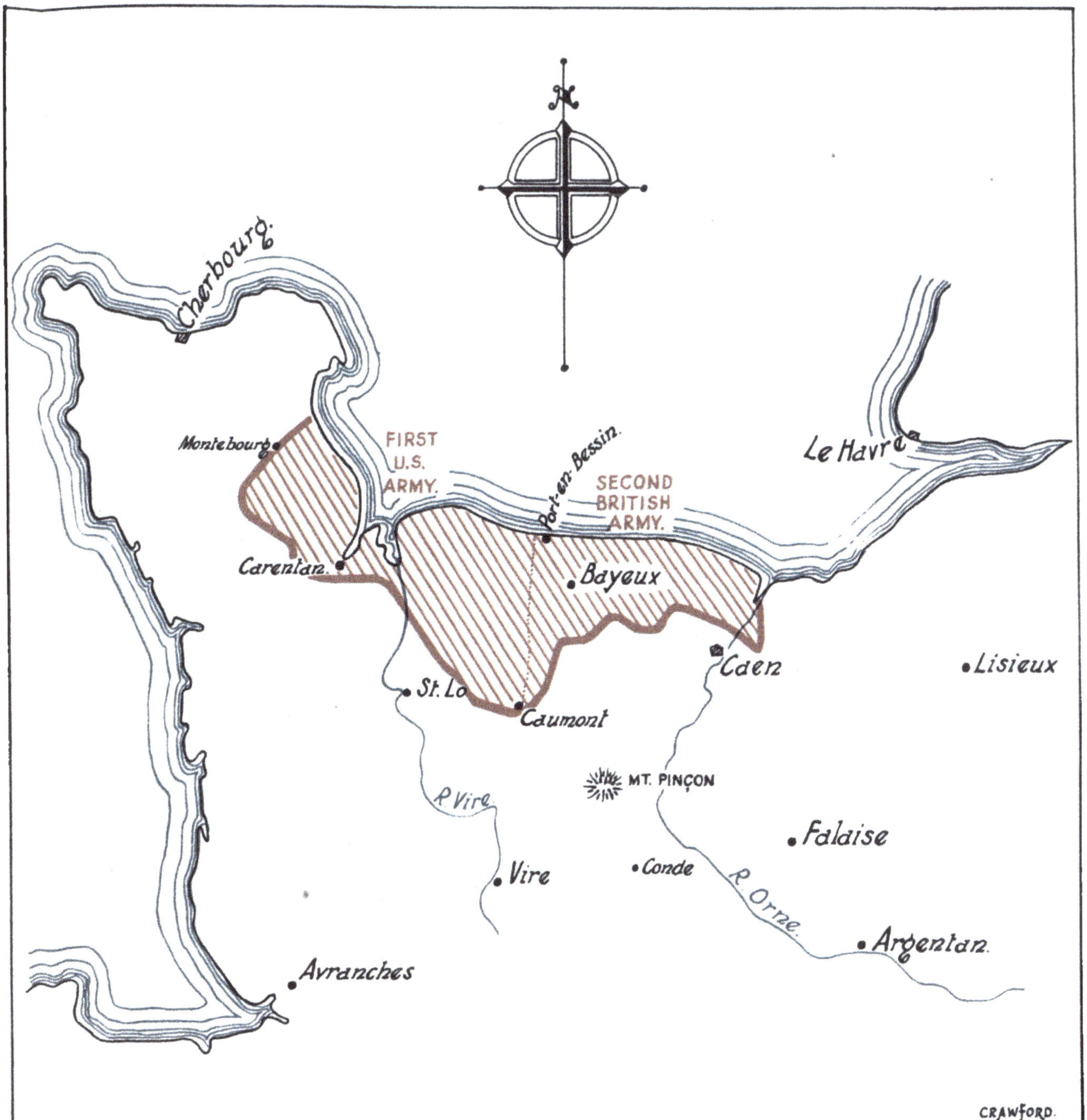

THE NORMANDY COAST
SHOWING POSITIONS HELD AT 15 JUNE 1945.
Scale - 1:1,000,000.

MAP 1.

MAP 2

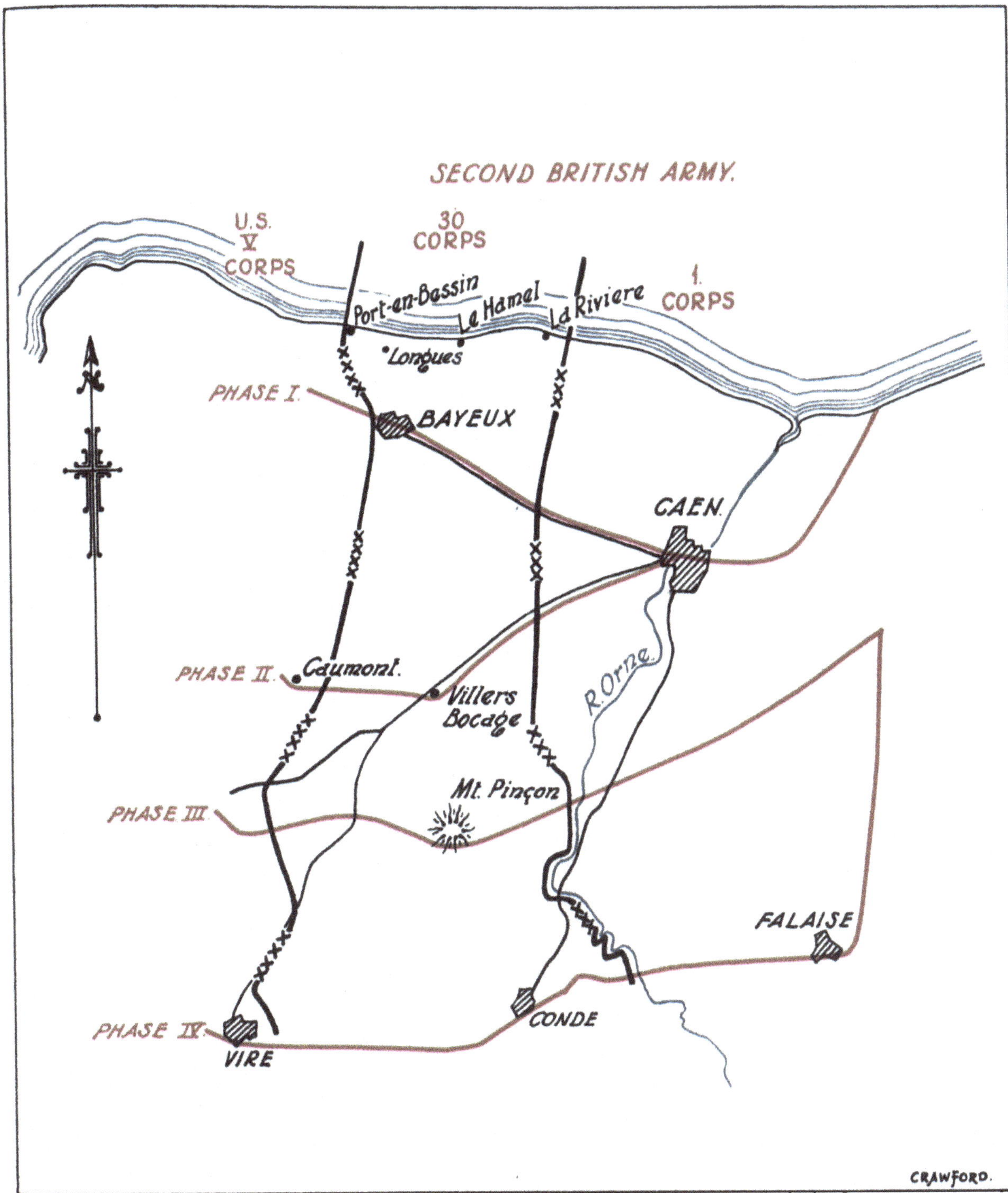

THE SECOND ARMY PLAN.

Scale - 1:500,000.

0 5 10 15 20

•Miles•

MAP 2.

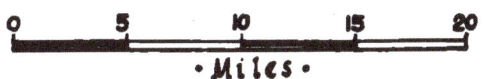

Opposition from enemy coast defence batteries was negligible; only one battery in fact engaged the craft on 30 Corps' beaches. The Luftwaffe was conspicious by its absence, whereas our fighter cover was both extensive and continous. Impressive attacks by medium and heavy bombers were made against enemy strong-points during the morning.

The enemy opposition to the assault of 69 and 231 Inf Brigades was rather stiffer than had been predicted. Three German battalions were, in fact, encountered where only one had been expected. Two of these were low category troops of 716 Inf Div and did not offer prolonged resistance, but a battalion of 352 Inf Div was made of better stuff and held out in the Le Hamel locality until noon. The delay imposed by this battalion slowed down the landing of the reserve brigades. In consequence the initial objectives were not entirely gained although by nightfall the leading troops had penetrated about five miles inland from the beaches and had approached within some two miles of Bayeux. The 47 (RM) Commando had reached a point about three miles east of their objective, Port en Bessin.

Casualties had been considerably lighter than anticipated.

On the left flank, 1 Corps had been engaged in heavy fighting with 21 Pz Div but their airborne troops had succeeded in making a bridgehead over the river Orne. On the right, the US forces had only gained a precarious foothold on the beaches, their deepest penetration only reaching some 3,000 yards inland.

On 7 June, enemy resistance on the Corps front was light compared with D Day and by noon the original beachhead line had been secured. During the afternoon, 50 (N) Div entered Bayeux and 47 (RM) Commando captured Port en Bessin and the coast battery at Longues with some 200 prisoners. By nightfall, forward troops had crossed the Bayeux—Caen road and all the "D Day objectives" had been secured. 7 Armd Div, the first armoured division to land in France, started to disembark on 7 June.

Tac HQ 30 Corps was established at Meuvaines at 2200 hrs 7 June.

Meanwhile the main enemy effort was directed against 1 Corps front, where a tank battle was fought against 21 Pz Div north of Caen On the right, V US Corps considerably improved its positions.

The next eight days were spent in consolidating the beachhead positions, against which the Germans gradually built up their strength.

It was clear that whereas their first task was to seal it off, they hoped eventually to drive it in. On the east, their main efforts were directed to holding the Caen pivot and to attacking with increasing vigour the 30 Corps penetrations between Caen and Bayeux. On the west, they attempted to prevent the Americans cutting off the Cotentin peninsula.

On 8 and 9 June, the effect of the enemy build up on the Corps front was reflected in the stiff resistance which met the attempts of 50 (N) Div to reach Villers Bocage. Nevertheless, Sully was reached by a westward thrust on 7 June and contact was made with 1 US Div on the Corps right on the 9th. On this day, the first enemy tanks were seen and knocked out. These belonged to Pz Lehr Div, wich had been committed by the enemy to fill the gap which the Corps was forcing open between 352 Inf Div and 12 SS Pz Div. During the day, all the ground north of the Bayeux—Caen road was cleared and, with the capture of St Pierre by 50 (N) Div, control was secured of the important lateral road from Caen to Balleroy. On the Corps flanks, 1 US Div had made good progress reaching the Bayeux—St Lo road, but on the left 1 Corps had been unable to capture Caen, where the enemy armour was counter-attacking without respite.

There now followed a succession of attacks launched against Tilly by 7 Armd Div, which had taken over the left sector of the Corps front. By nightfall 10 June its leading troops had reached within one mile of the village and early the following morning succeeded in getting a footing in its northern outskirts. But the Bocage was difficult tank country and enemy infantry were able to stalk our tanks at close range with Panzerfausts and to snipe into the open turret hatches. Throughout 11 June Pz Lehr Div threw in a series of local counter attacks and by evening succeeded in forcing 7 Armd Div to withdraw from the village.

On the Corps right front, 50 (N) Div managed to capture La Belle Epine. Meanwhile on the right flank, V US Corps had been making excellent progress and were heading for Caumont. Advantage was therefore taken of this success; 7 Armd Div was pulled out from the hotly contested Tilly area and was ordered to put in a "right hook" with the object of capturing Villers Bocage from the west. 50 (N) Div was to hold the Corps left flank.

In spite of several spoiling attacks by the enemy, the 7 Armd Div thrust started well and by midnight on 12 June its leading troops were

MAP 3

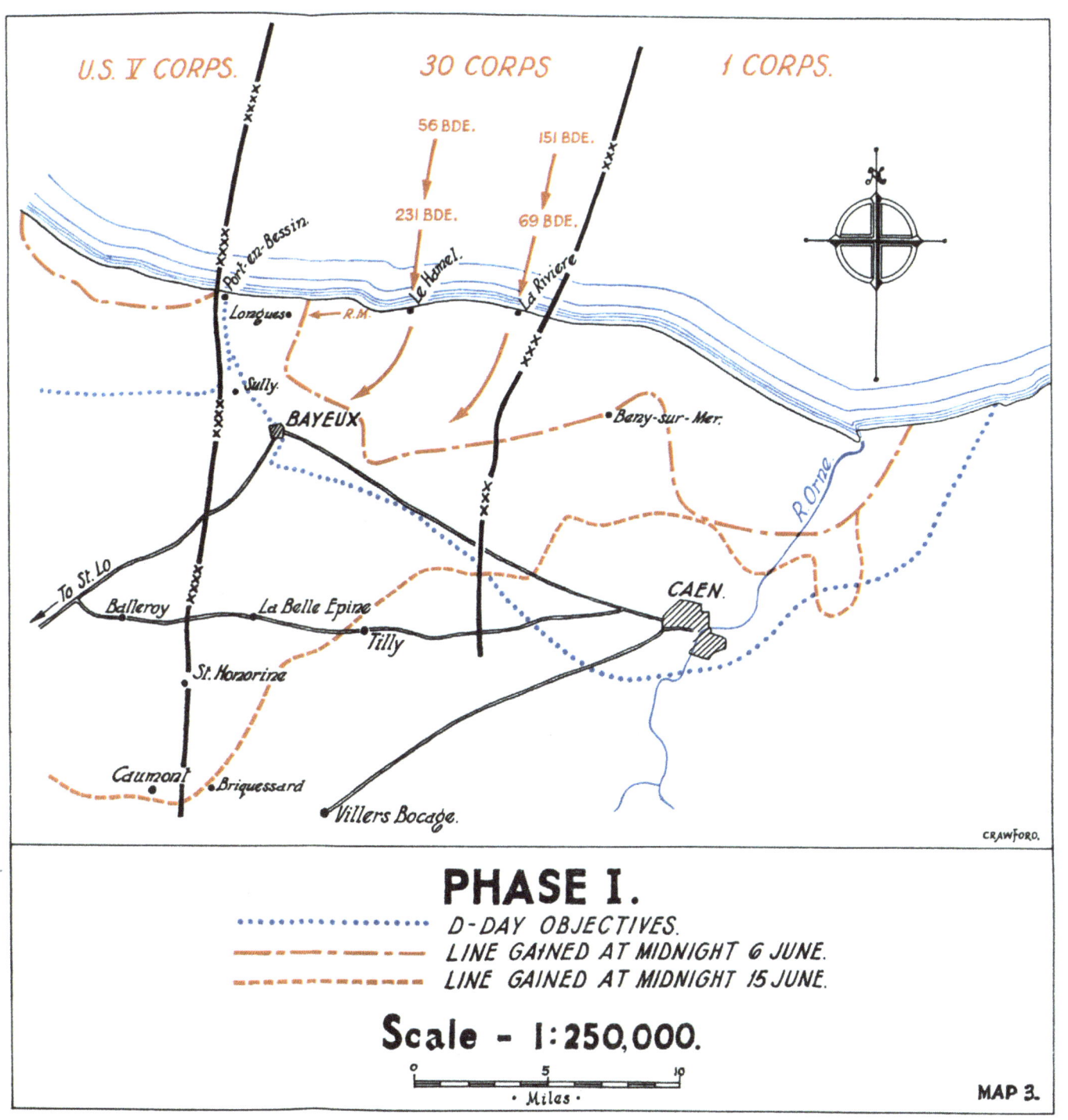

MAP 4

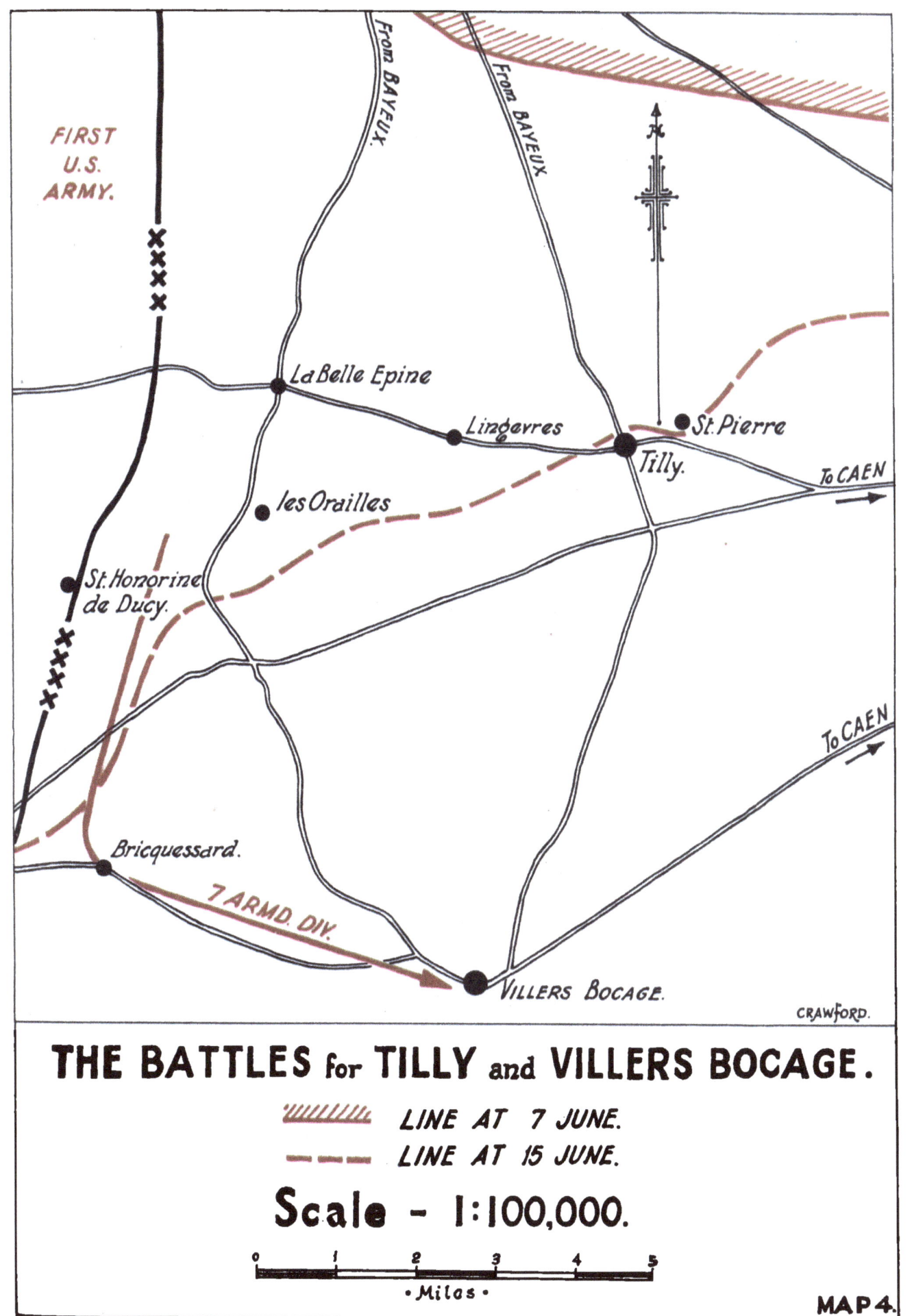

THE BATTLES for TILLY and VILLERS BOCAGE.

▨▨▨ LINE AT 7 JUNE.
––––– LINE AT 15 JUNE.

Scale - 1:100,000.

MAP 4.

reported in Bricquessard. It completed its outflanking movement the following morning and its leading tanks entered Villers at 0845 hrs 13 June, the infantry moving in shortly afterwards. By now the enemy was thoroughly alarmed by this thrust to the left flank of his Caen defences and he re-acted quickly, directing a fresh panzer div (2 Pz Div) to the Villers area. That afternoon he mounted a counter attack with some 40 Tiger and Mk. IV tanks. Infantry and tanks, under cover of a smoke screen, approached the village from the south and tanks operated round its northern outskirts. In spite of intervention by all our artillery which could bear, the enemy attack made progress and by nightfall 7 Armd Div had been forced to withdraw about 2 miles to the west of Villers.

On 14 June, 50 (N) Div supported by the Corps artillery and by the guns of V US Corps attacked towards Villers from the north and made some headway, against strong resistance, to reach the Tilly— La Belle Epine road. On the Corps right front an enemy counter attack with some 20 tanks was repulsed by 7 Armd Div, with heavy losses to the enemy. At least 10 Tigers and Panthers were knocked out and many enemy troops were killed. 49 Div, which had now landed, was directed to take over the left sector of the Corps front. On 15 June, 7 Armd Div was withdrawn from its exposed position west of Villers to the area of St Honorine de Ducy—Bricquessard whilst 50 (N) Div continued its advance southward and reached Les Orailles.

The 15 June was notable for a magnificent action fought by 8 Armd Bde which was supporting 50 (N) Div. Whilst protecting our infantry consolidating in Lingèvres, the leading Armd Squadron observed a number of enemy tanks approaching the village. They were immediately engaged by our leading "Firefly" and two enemy tanks were accounted for in as many minutes. The tanks then closed to within 100 yards of each other and the leading British tank received a direct hit with AP, all the crew except one being wounded. The gunner, who had not been hurt, collected a fire extinguisher and put out the fire which was beginning to brew up in the gear box, and then carried the unconscious driver and co-driver safely to a nearby church. Throughout this period he was under direct fire from very close range and his tank was being continuously shot at, until finally it burned completely out. In the afternoon this same Squadron was again engaged in close fighting with enemy tanks and no less than four German tanks were knocked out at a range of 400 yards, without loss to ourselves. Thus the Squadron's score for the day was six Panthers destroyed for the loss of one Sherman.

By 15 June, the first phase of Operation Overlord was completed. 21 Army Group had obtained a firm lodgement on the Continent and its gradual build-up within the beachhead was progressing satisfactorily. However, the enemy had correctly appreciated the importance of holding Caen, Carentan and Montebourg and by his fierce defence of these key-points, he had denied the Americans and British the use of both Cherbourg and Caen. In this task he had commited no less than twelve Divisions, including one Para and five Panzer Divisions. But the majority of his counter attacks had been beaten off and heavy casualties had been inflicted on some of his best troops and equipment. Second Army had captured some 5,000 prisoners and 30 Corps alone had knocked out seventy of his most modern tanks.

The Development of the Beachhead (Map 8)

During this phase, the Commander-in-Chief's plan continued relentlessly to draw the German reserves to the Normandy front, as a preliminary to their defeat west of the Seine. The enemy was particularly sensitive to any offensive south or east from Caen; a fact which the Commander-in-Chief exploited to the utmost. By continuing to attack in these Sectors, General Montgomery drew more and more enemy reserves to this part of the front, thus preparing an opening on the American sector, where he intended the eventual break-through to come.

At this time 7 Armd Div was standing firm on the right of the 30 Corps front, with 50 (N) Div and 49 Div pressing south and southeast towards Tilly and Christot. On 16 June, 49 Div captured the heavily booby-trapped villages of Bronay and Christot, where there were many SS corpses. Small gains only were made on 17 June. On the right, 50 (N) Div advanced to within half-a-mile of Tilly and on the left 49 Div made some local advances and repelled a series of counter attacks. Within a period of 3 hours in the late evening, three attacks supported by tanks were launched against them, but these were all broken up by our artillery fire and at least two Tigers and one Panther were knocked out.

MAP 5

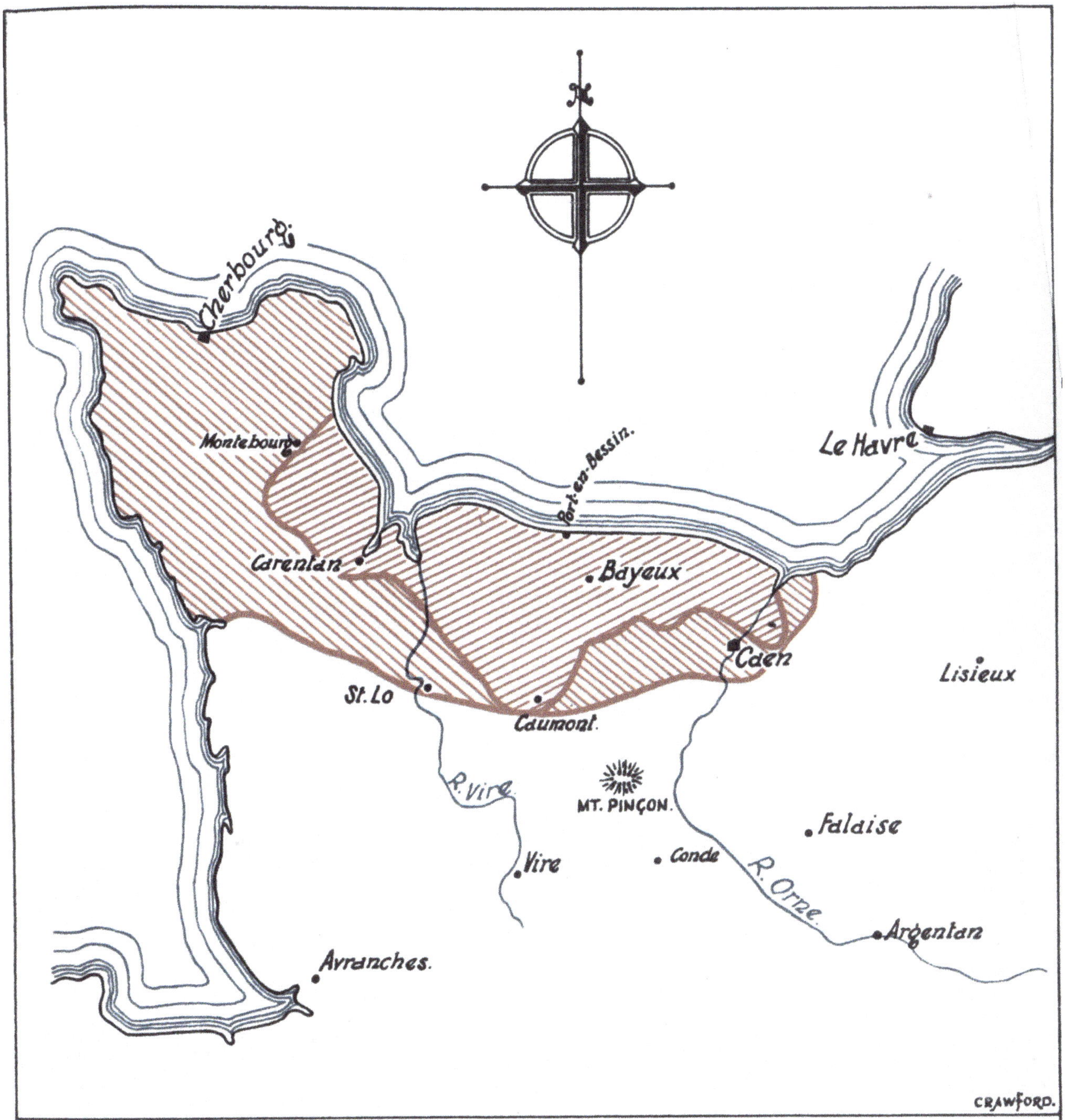

THE DEVELOPMENT of the BEACH-HEAD.

GROUND GAINED AT 15 JUNE.
GROUND GAINED 15 JUNE – 24 JULY.

Scale – 1:1,000,000.

· Miles ·

MAP 5.

By 18 June, the Battle of Tilly, which had been raging for 9 days, was almost over. The village was now practically surrounded by 50 (N) Div on the north and west and by 49 Div in the east. It fell on 19 June and later that day, troops of 50 (N) Div, knocking out five enemy tanks and two SP guns, gained a footing in the outskirts of Hottot. The division was supported in this action by HMS RODNEY which shelled Hottot at extreme range. Throughout the next few days, heavy enemy counter attacks supported by unusually strong concentrations of artillery prevented either 49 or 50 (N) Divs from making any significant progress and their precarious grip on Hottot could not be consolidated. The enemy had reacted strongly to the southward advance by the Corps and had switched many of his armoured reserves. including elements of 1 SS Corps, 12 SS Pz Div and 21 Pz Div, to meet it.

During the period 22/24 June, large scale re-grouping took place in Second Army and 8 Corps was interposed in the line between 1 and 30 Corps.

As soon as this was completed, 8 Corps was to attack eastwards to seize crossings over the river Odon southwest of Caen. Immediately before the 8 Corps attack, 30 Corps was to attack on its left front to secure the area Noyers and exploit towards Aunay. This task was allotted to 49 Div and their first bound was the general line Juvigny—Rauray.

The 30 Corps attack started through a thick ground mist at 0415 hrs 25 June. The enemy's reaction was at first weak and the customary counter attacks were not developed. 49 Div captured the village of Fontenay by midnight and, conforming on the right 50 (N) Div made some ground south of Tilly. The following day, two regiments of 8 Armd Brigade, with one battalion of 49 Div under command, resumed the attack. But the enemy resistance was extremely stiff and at least 30 enemy tanks were encountered in the area. It was therefore decided later in the day that 49 Div should launch a fresh attack from the north and by last light, one battalion had reached the outskirts of Rauray. About ten enemy tanks had been destroyed.

50 (N) Div captured Juvigny and Rauray was finally cleared on 27 June. Meanwhile, 8 Corps had gained a bridgehead over the Odon, northeast of Gavrus. During three days' fighting, sixty German tanks had been knocked out in the attacks by 8 and 30 Corps. On 28 June, 49 Div continued their attack and entered Brettevillette

against strong opposition but, during the afternoon, a fierce counter attack by 2 SS Pz Div re-took the village. This enemy division had been rushed from St Lo to meet the threat of the 30 Corps advance.

At this stage, the Second Army was holding all the enemy armour on the Normandy front (Map 6). From this it was clear that the enemy was seeking to fight a decisive battle west of the river Orne, but heavy losses had already been inflicted on the enemy in casualties to both men and equipment. It was estimated that since D Day he had lost no less than 90,000 men, including nine generals, and of the 360 tanks destroyed by Second Army at this point, 30 Corps could lay claim to more than one third.

Cherbourg had surrendered with a great number of prisoners to First US Army on 27 June.

At the end of June it became necessary to obliterate Villers Bocage and Aunay-sur-Odon, two small towns which were key points in the road-network on our immediate front. The bomber's job was done with terrifying efficiency and no one who saw the results will ever forget it. The sacrifice of Aunay, in particular, — one shattered church spire was all that remained standing — was proved not to be in vain, for the Germans never attempted to use its vital roads again.

July opened with a fury of counter attacks on the Corps sector*, the enemy employing all his armour and SS formations in an endeavour to cut through the salient, which 8 and 30 Corps were beginning to thrust southwards. On 1 July the enemy put in his greatest offensive since the invasion began and no less than four counter attacks were repulsed within 24 hours, south of Rauray, by 49 Div alone. Forty enemy tanks were knocked out on the Corps front that day. During the next few days many more counter attacks were held and driven back, the Corps artillery very often breaking up the attacks before they had time to develop. At this time also the Corps was gradually beginning to develop that dominance over the enemy artillery which it was rarely to lose in the future.

On 8 July, 1 Corps launched an attack, which was preceded by very heavy bombing, on Caen. Simultaneously, 50 (N) Div attacked in the area Bois St Germain and by dusk had reached the Caumont—Caen road. The next day the usual counter attacks were staged and repulsed;

---

* On 1 July, 7 Armd Div was withdrawn to Army reserve from the Corps right sector, its front being taken over by V US Corps.

MAP 6

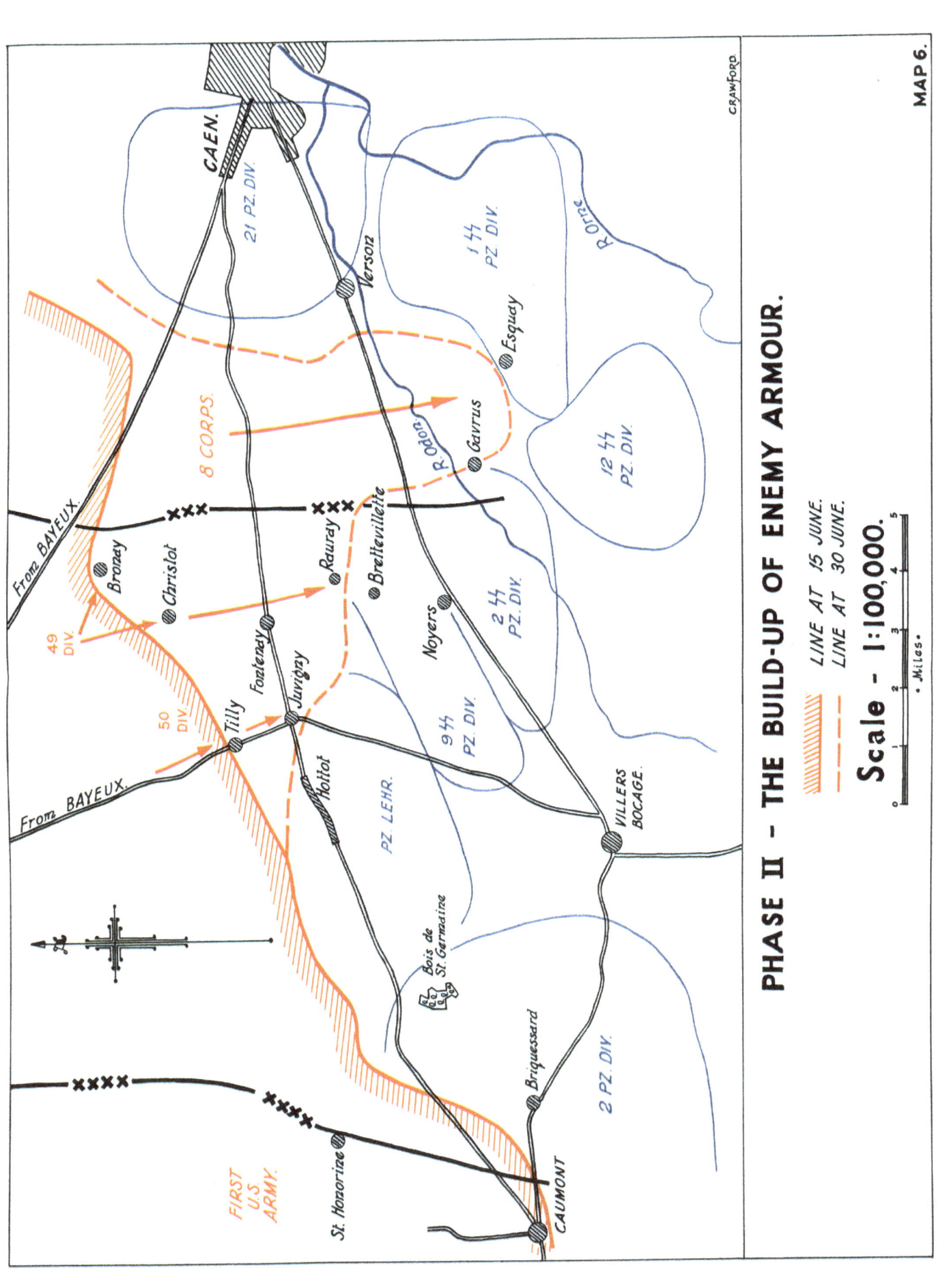

eleven German tanks were knocked out and the 50 (N) Div position remained firm. On 11 July, 231 Inf Bde of 50 (N) Div put in a thrust on the left flank towards Hottot and, taking 60 prisoners, reached the outskirts of the village. By now 1 Corps had cleared all of Caen west of the river Orne and there then followed a lull on the whole of Second Army front.

Meanwhile on the right the Americans were making excellent progress and had crossed the river Vire and were threatening St Lo. To meet this threat, the enemy was beginning to switch his armour westwards and gradually the armoured formations which had been so vigorously opposing the Corps were replaced by infantry (Map 7).

The offensive was resumed by Second Army in mid July. 12 Corps, which had taken over from 8 Corps in the centre, attacked on 15 July and seized Gavrus. The offensive was extended to the 30 Corps front the following day when 59 Div (which had now joined the Corps) attacked and gained a footing on the high ground south of Brettevillette. 300 prisoners, mostly from 277 Inf Div were captured during the day. The attack was continued on 17 July and throughout the day 59 Div was engaged in heavy fighting on the outskirts of Noyers, into which the enemy had moved tanks and fresh infantry. By last light, our troops were still outside the village.

On 18 July, preceded by a tremendous air attack by over 3,200 bombers, Second Army launched an offensive from their Orne bridgehead and succeded in breaking through the enemy positions southeast of Caen. This attack had repercussions on the Corps front and the enemy was found to be evacuating his positions. 50 (N) Div followed up this withdrawal and occupied Hottot, taking well over 300 prisoners. By 20 July, the line had reached almost to the Bois St Germain and St Vaast.

Thus ended the second phase of the fighting on the Continent *. Caen had been cleared of the enemy and a secure left pivot had thereby been secured for the Allies. On the right the Cotentin peninsula had been practically occupied. During these operations, many enemy formations had been pinned down in the centre and, in a period of constant fighting, had suffered crippling casualties. Since D Day, 12,000 prisoners had been taken and 700 tanks had been destroyed on the front of Second Army.

---

* The following changes in the Corps Order of Battle took place at the end of July:

15 (S) Div came under command and took over the Caumont sector from V US Corps. On 29 July it passed to command 8 Corps.

49 Div passed to command 1 Corps.

59 Div passed to command 12 Corps.

The beachhead area had been developed and the initiative had gradually been wrested from the enemy. 21 Army Group now stood ready to exploit its period of hard fighting and to break through into the heart of France.

The Breakthrough to the Seine

For fifty days, the British and American armies had been fighting for position in the fields of France. The great port of Cherbourg would soon be working and a strong pivot had been gained at Caen. The original plans for exploitation were therefore put into effect. First US Army was to clear the Cotentin peninsula and then swing its right flank eastwards and southwards towards Alencon; meanwhile unrelenting pressure was to be kept up against the enemy by Second British and First Canadian * Armies to prevent him releasing any troops for action against the Americans. The immediate task of the British Army was to attack the enemy south of Caumont and to prevent him using the Mont Pincon feature as a pivot for withdrawal in face of the Americans.

On 25 July, two big attacks, both preceded by heavy air bombardments, were made on the flanks of 30 Corps. On the right the American Army launched an offensive west of the river Vire and on the left the Canadians attacked east of the Orne.

Meanwhile preparations were made for 30 Corps** to advance southwards on 30 July and capture Bois du Homme feature, southwest of Jurques. 43 Div was given this task and was then to protect the Corps right flank by securing the high ground in the area Ondefontaine. 50 (N) Div was to advance on the left to secure the feature south of Amaye-sur-Seulles. 7 Armd Div was held in reserve with a view to exploitation. The right flank was to be protected by 8 Corps who were to capture Sept Vents and Les Logues and to exploit to the southwest.

When dawn broke on 30 July heavy clouds scudded over the sky and the weather did not bid fair for the air attack which was to open the Corps' assault. But flying very low and often swooping down to almost zero feet, 700 heavy bombers rained down nearly 4,000 tons of bombs on the enemy facing the 8 and 30 Corps fronts. When the infantry of 50 (N) Div attacked, however, they met considerable opposition from heavily defended positions on their front, and, in spite of the support from bombers and artillery, they could make little

---

* First Canadian Army had taken over the 1 Corps front on 23 July 44.
** 30 Corps now consisted of 7 Armd, 43 and 50 (N) Divs.

MAP 7

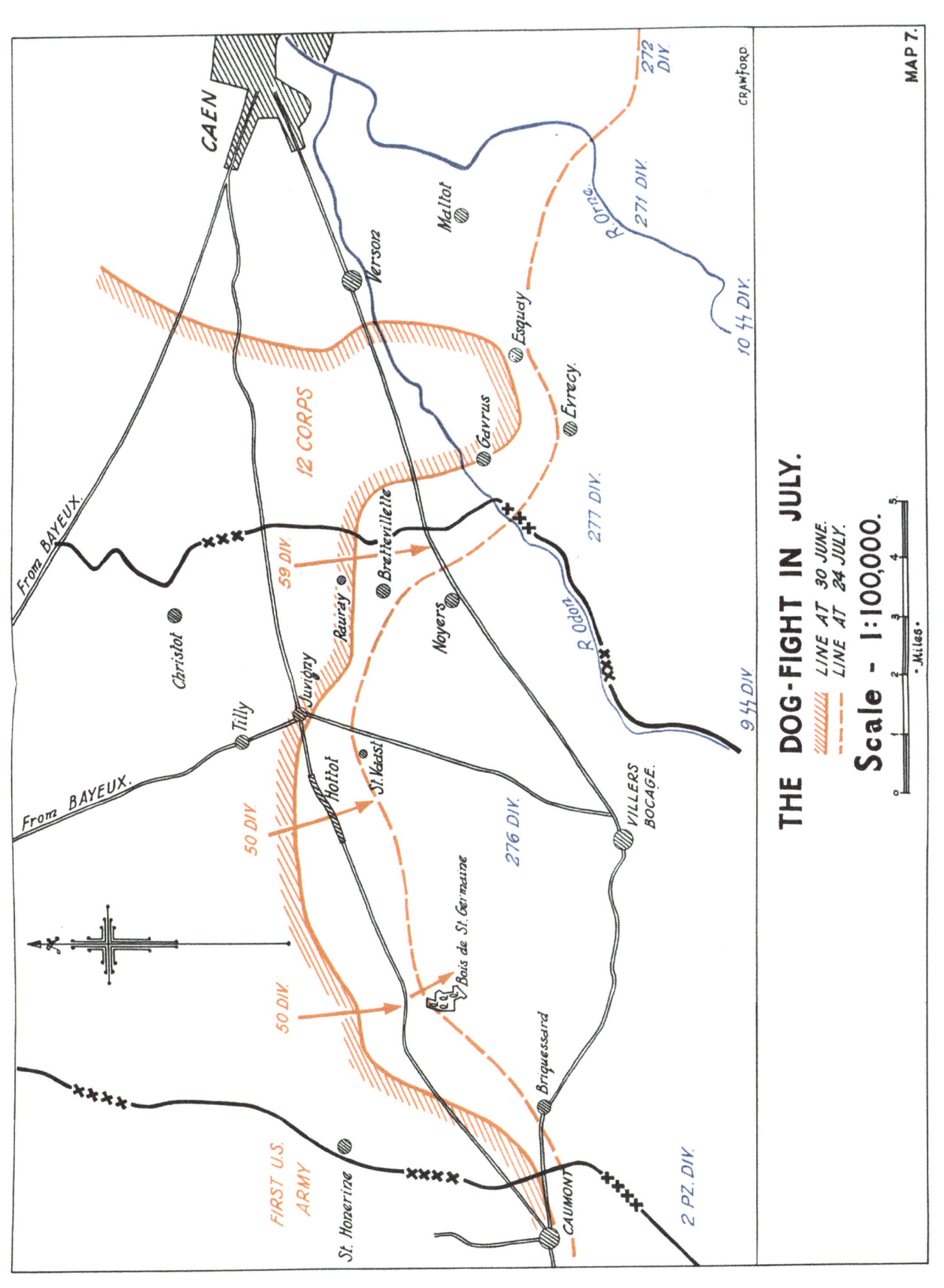

MAP 8

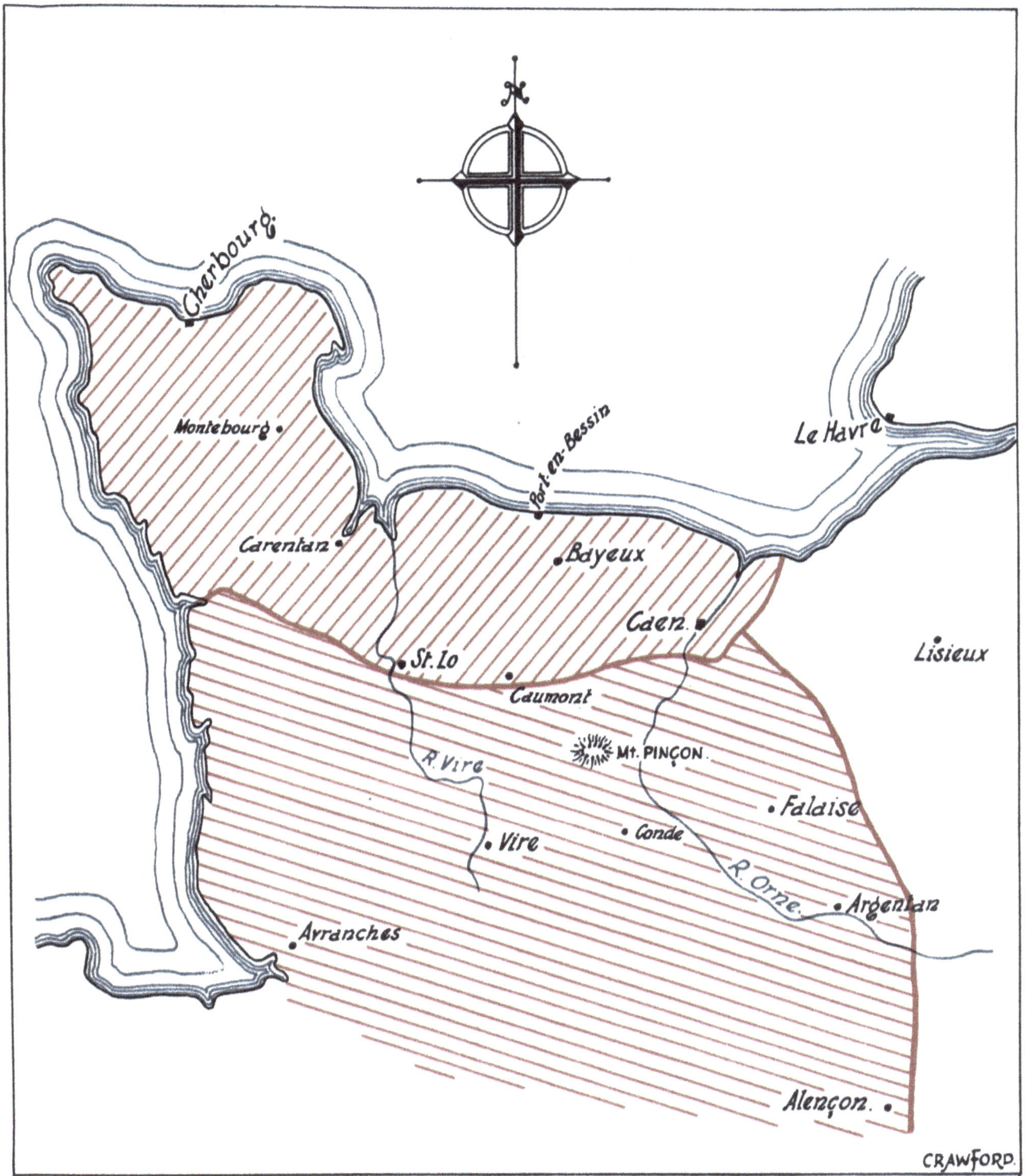

THE BREAKTHROUGH TO FALAISE.

 GROUND GAINED AT 24 JULY.
GROUND GAINED 24 JULY – 19 AUG.

Scale – 1:1,000,000.

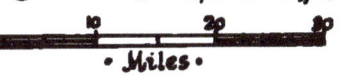

MAP 8.

progress south of the stream, which ran across their divisional front. The enemy had taken full advantage of the static period in this sector and had laid a multitude of mines and booby traps, which proved a tremendous handicap to the advancing troops. On the right, 43 Div fared better and making a detour round Bricquessard, it managed to establish itself on the high ground just north of Cahagnes. 200 prisoners were taken by the Corps that day.

The following day was more successful. 50 (N) Div captured St Germain d'Ectot and Orbois and 43 Div cleared Cahagnes and pushed on to St Pierre du Fresne. A further 200 prisoners were taken and more than 100 enemy dead were found in Cahagnes alone. On the right flank, the armour of 8 Corps had reached the Foret l'Eveque. Further to the right, the Americans captured Avranches and the gateway to their exploitation in France was opened.

On 1 August, after very heavy fighting, 43 Div managed to scale the wooded slopes of the Bois du Homme feature, and by 2000 hrs two Bns of 214 Inf Brigade had reached its summit which towered 1,000 feet above the surrounding country. That afternoon, 7 Armd Div was passed through preparatory to attacking Aunay sur Odon the next day and by dusk its leading troops had reached Breuil. Simultaneously 43 Div. was to advance to Ondefontaine and 50 (N) Div to Amaye. The attack by 7 Armd Div on 2 August made little progress and failed to get nearer than two miles to the village. The infantry divisions, on the other hand, made good progress and between them captured nearly 500 prisoners. 43 Div captured Jurques and L'Oisonnière and established themselves firmly on the high ground west of Ondefontaine, while 50 (N) Div reached Amaye and advanced to the line of the river Seulles.

Throughout 3 August, there was bitter fighting all along the Corps front and many counter attacks were repulsed. 7 Armd Div did not take Aunay. On 4 August the enemy withdrew slightly and vacated Villers Bocage which was occupied by 50 (N) Div. On the right flank 43 Div. pushed south into Le Mesnil Auzouf and contacted 8 Corps. Aunay was not captured until 5 August.

Lieut General B. G. Horrocks CB., DSO., MC., took over command of 30 Corps from Lieut General G. C. Bucknall CB., MC., on 4 August 1944.

Meanwhile the American columns were pressing into France from the Contentin peninsula. To meet this threat, the enemy denuded his 15 Army, north of the Seine, of all its armour and all its first class infantry. The German forces in the West had been drawn into a 'killing ground' prescribed by Field Marshal Montgomery. The battle now proceeded to their final annihilation. Second British Army was directed at this time to pivot on its left flank and to advance southeast towards Thury Harcourt and Argentan. The immediate task allotted to 30 Corps, in the centre of the Second Army front, was to secure Mont Pincon and to capture Conde sur Noireau.

There were no illusions over the difficulty of assaulting the massive Mont Pincon, which rose to some 1,200 feet above the undulating country to the north. Its northern slopes were steep and it had long been prepared by the enemy as the key to an important defence line. Its capture was to be the task of 43 Div supported by 8 Armd Brigade, whilst 7 Armd Div was to be prepared to move round on the left flank. 50 (N) Div remained in Corps reserve.

The assault started, under cover of a barrage, in the afternoon of 6 August. After initial setbacks, the leading tanks of 8 Armd Brigade outstripped the leading infantry and swarmed slowly to the summit before nightfall. During the night, our infantry established a footing on the mountain and stood ready to repel the expected counter attack. But, except for some rather intense shelling, the enemy made no real effort to recapture Mont Pincon and on 7 August, 43 Div, after heavy hand-to-hand fighting, was able to force its way into Plessis at the southern foot of the feature. To the east of Pincon, 7 Armd Div attacked up the escarpment and made some ground on the left flank. During the past 48 hours, 430 prisoners had been taken.

At first light on 8 August, the attack was resumed with 7 Armd Div leading and 50 (N) Div following up. In spite of the loss of Mont Pincon itself, the enemy appeared to be determined to hold on to his positions at all costs, and 7 Armd Div was held up by several anti-tank guns. Further west, 43 Div was fully engaged in mopping up the orchards and villages just south of the high ground.

There were now signs on the Corps front that the enemy was starting to crack. In order to maintain unremitting pressure on the enemy it was necessary to concentrate the maximum forces into the

MAP 9

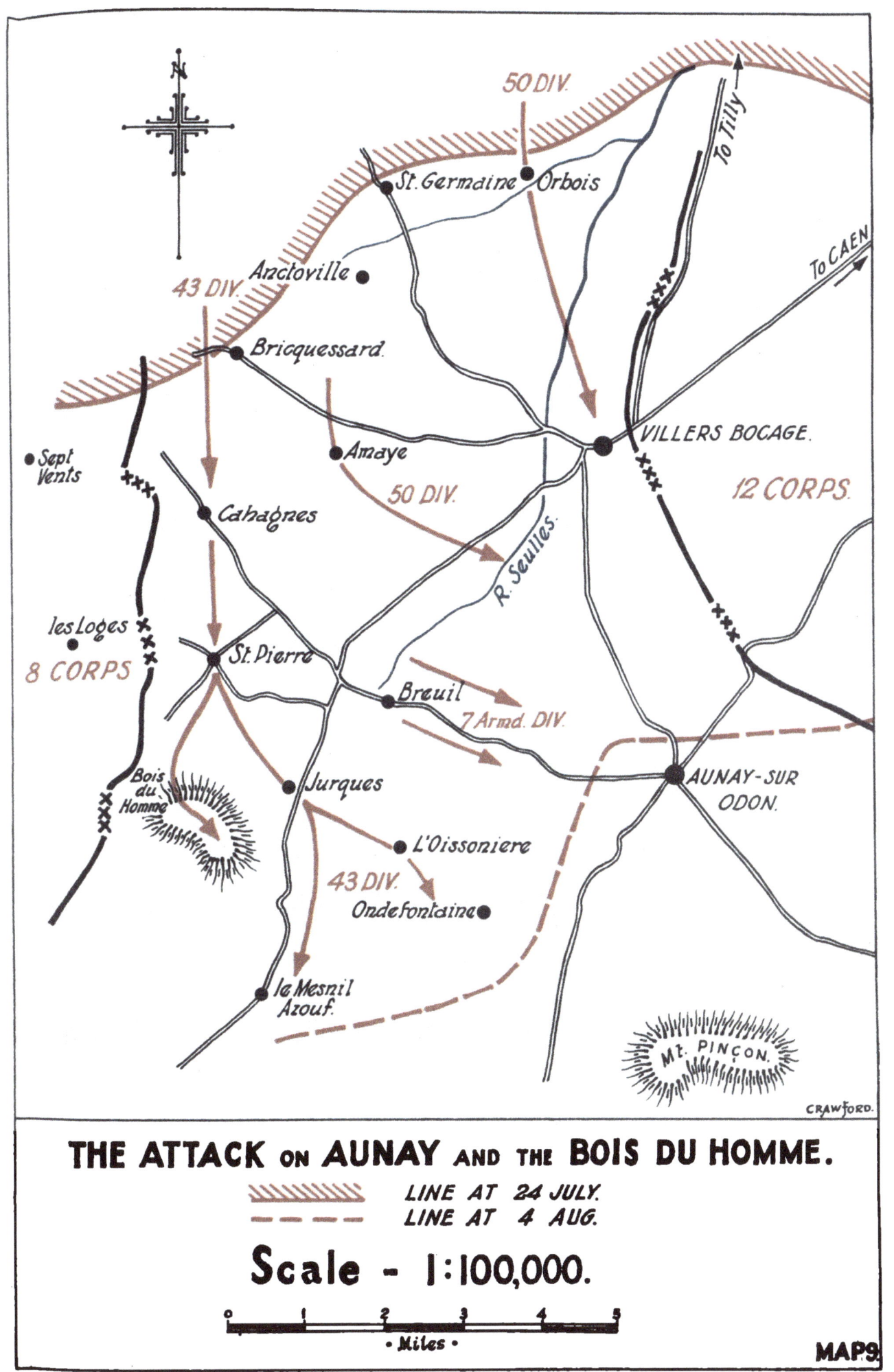

sectors where the attack was to be pressed home. Risks had to be taken by holding other sectors very lightly; at one stage the greater part of the Corps front was held by recce regiments. Each Division in turn was pulled out for short rests of two or three days; thus comparatively fresh troops were always available to maintain the momentum of the attack. It was due to this and to the excellence of the artillery support that the German resistance was gradually worn down.

The attack on 30 Corps front was resumed shortly after midday on 9 August by 50 (N) Div. They met heavy mortar and artillery fire on the road from Pincon to Conde, but by last light had established themselves on the high ground east of Crapouville. During the day, 400 prisoners were taken, bringing the number captured by 30 Corps since 30 July up to 2,200. For the next three days 50 (N) Div made dogged progress towards Conde against stiff resistance: each day a few kilometres were gained and about 200 prisoners were taken. On 13 August, 50 (N) Div was withdrawn to reserve and 43 Div continued to advance to Conde. On the following day, 43 Div captured Proussy and closed to within two miles of Conde.

Away to the south, the Third US Army was making great progress and was reported to be advancing from Alencon towards Sées and Carrouges. Meanwhile the enemy at Mortain had been decisively repulsed and was in danger of encirclement by the British and American armies heading towards Falaise. It now became evident that the enemy, reacting to this threat, had decided to withdraw on the Second Army front. 30 Corps was therefore given the role of pursuit Corps and, with 11 Armd Div under command *, was directed to push with all speed eastwards to Argentan.

Before daylight on 15 August, the enemy withdrew across the Noireau but they were quickly pursued. Attacking across the river, 43 Div succeeded in gaining a footing on the bank opposite Conde. On the right sector of the Corps front, 11 Armd Div secured Vassy. The next day progress was hampered by sharp resistance and many mines, but 43 Div pressed on to Berjou, while 11 Armd Div crossed the Noireau and reached the Flers—Conde road.

In spite of the dramatic events to the east, where the Canadians and Americans had almost closed the ring round the trapped enemy,

---

* 11 Armd Div had come under command 30 Corps from 8 Corps on 14 August. 7 Armd Div passed to command 1 Corps on 16 August.

the withdrawal on the 30 Corps front was comparatively orderly. On 17 August, 11 Armd Div overcoming pockets of paratroops who were determined to fight hard even though their link with the east was liable to be cut at any moment, reached Briouze and made contact with VII US Corps on the right flank. More than 400 prisoners were captured during the day, bringing the total taken by the Corps since 30 July to 4,200. On 18 August, 11 Armd Div, now leading the Corps advance, pressed on to Putanges and soon cleared the woods northeast of Ecouche, thus helping to compress the pocket of enemy to the east.

The pocket was in fact closed on 19 August by the joining of the V US Corps with the Polish Armd Div of the Canadian Army at Chambois. There then followed the destruction of all encircled enemy left in this cauldron. Assailed day and night by the Allied Air Forces and artillery, formation after formation was annihilated without quarter. On the "killing ground" of Chambois the remnants of the German Seventh Army were destroyed.

Meanwhile, far to the east the Americans had reached the Seine and had seized a bridgehead near Mantes Gassicourt. They were then ordered to thrust northwards along the west bank of the Seine, thereby carrying out a wide enveloping movement behind the disorganised enemy. At the same time, the Second British Army, with right 30 Corps and left 12 Corps, was ordered to pass through the forces holding the Chambois pocket and to advance to the Seine. 30 Corps was directed on Mantes Gassicourt.

"The swan" eastwards was continued by 11 Armd Div, with 50 (N) Div on the Corps left flank. Passing through Argentan and Gace, 11 Armd Div reached Laigle by 22 August, by which time 50 (N) Div had entered Touquettes. Shortly afterwards the Corps made contact with XIX US Corps, which was holding the west bank of the Seine and had reached as far north as Louviers and Elbeuf.

The past month had seen the heaviest defeat inflicted on the enemy. His losses in personnel and material had been enormous and it seemed doubtful if he could now marshal adequate forces even to hold the formidable Seine. On 24 August, 43 Div was ordered forward to the Rugles area preparatory to making an assault crossing over the river.

MAP 10

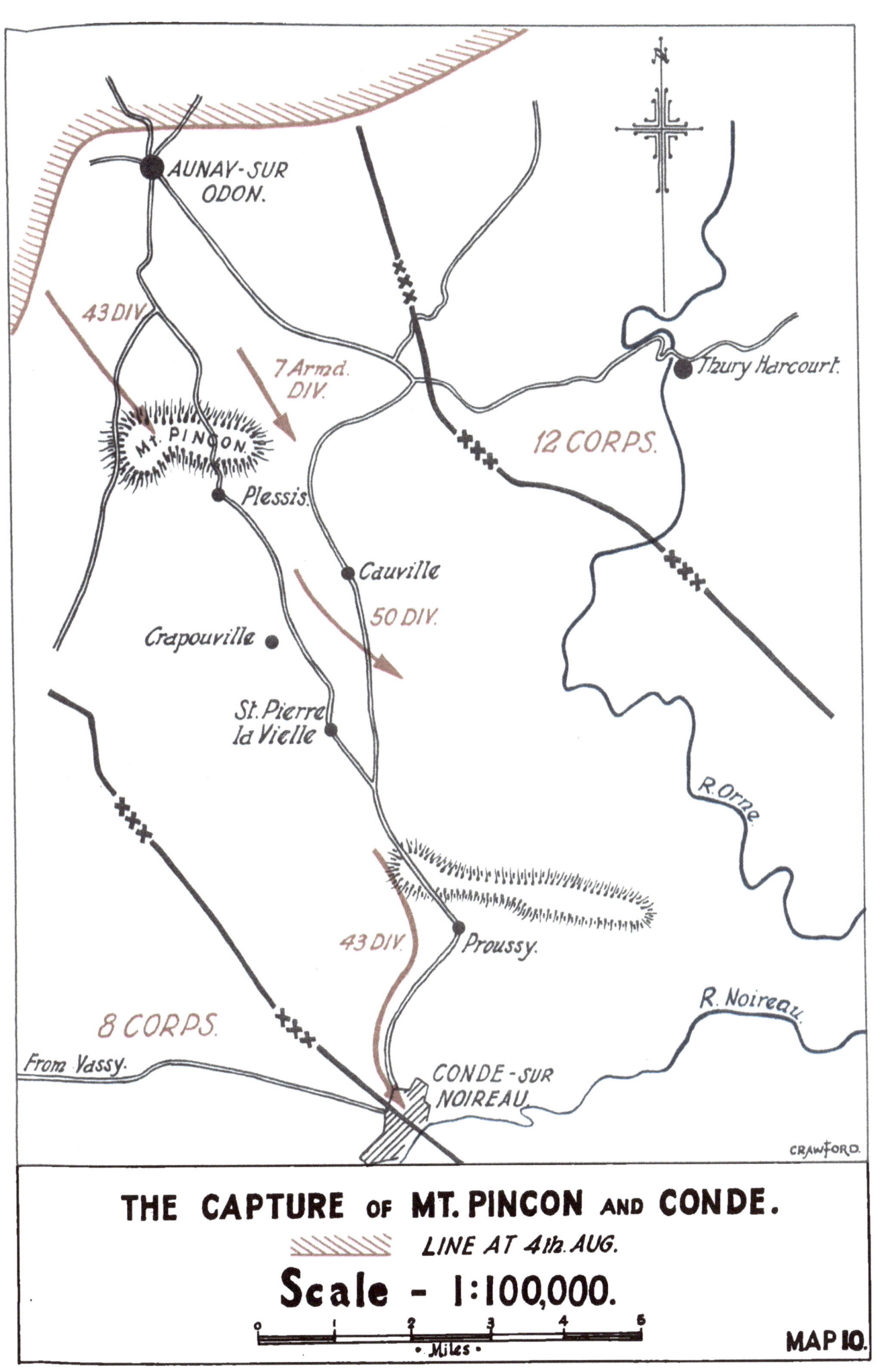

THE CAPTURE OF MT. PINCON AND CONDE.

LINE AT 4th. AUG.

Scale - 1:100,000.

MAP 10.

MAP 11

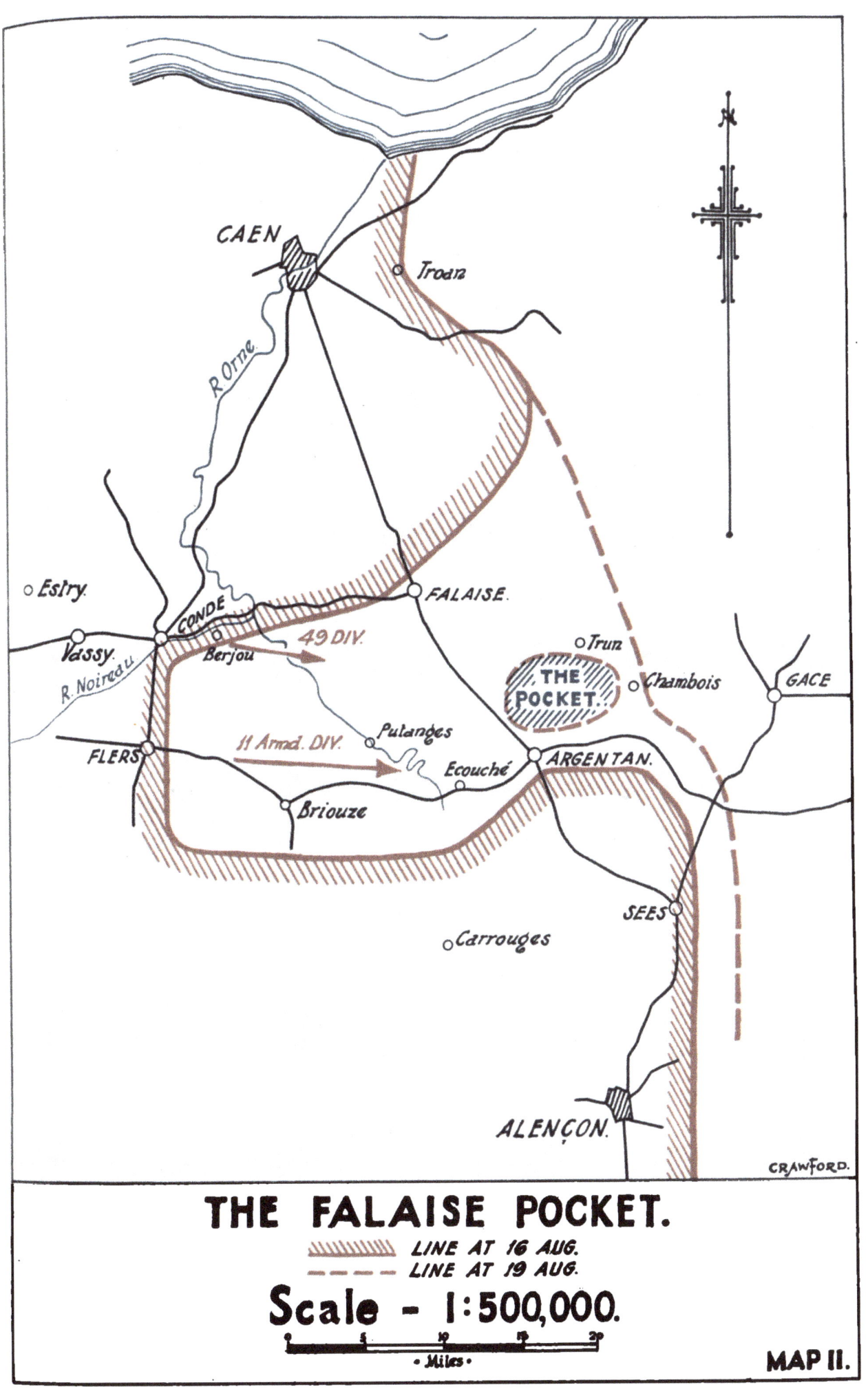

MAP 12

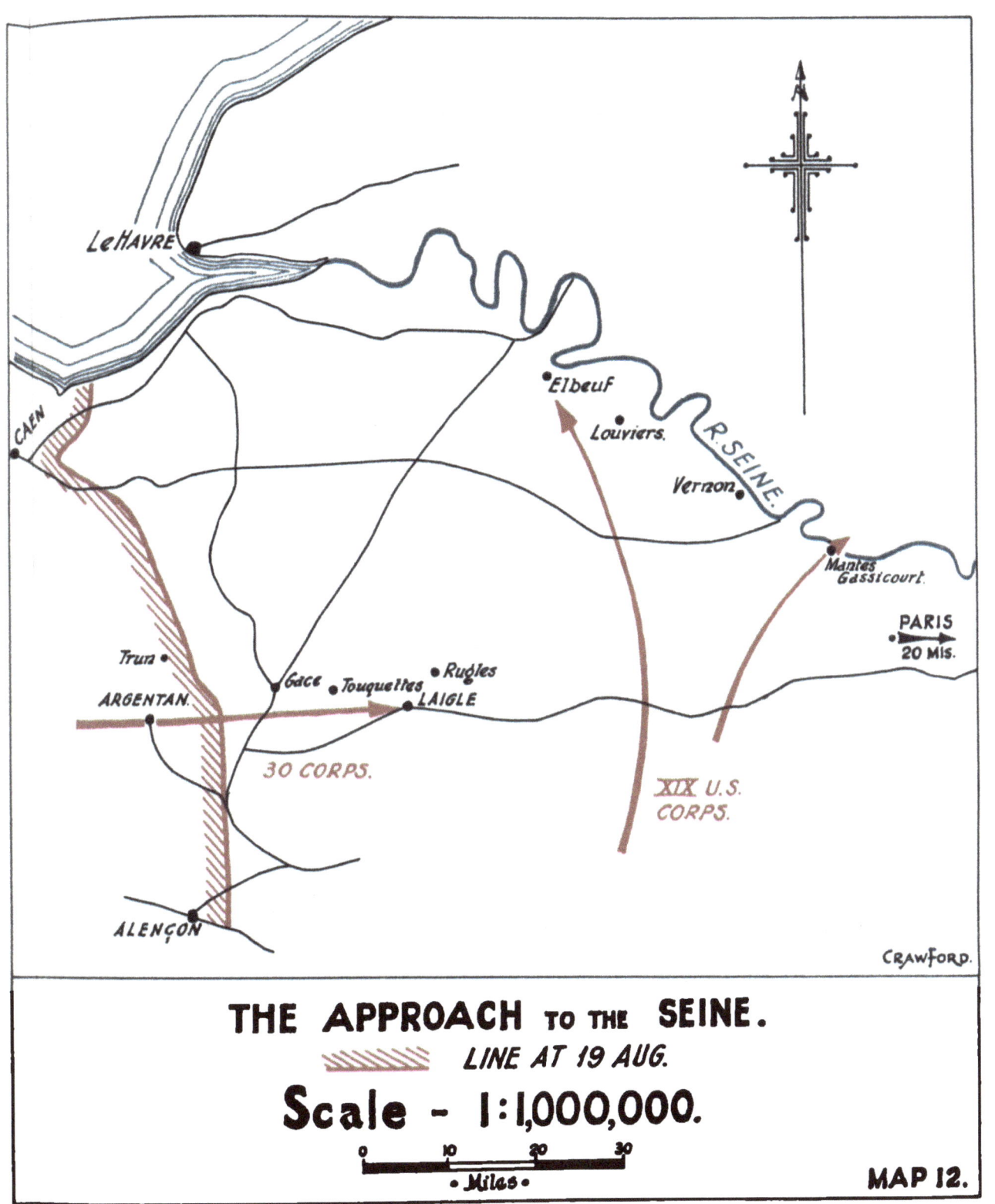

THE APPROACH TO THE SEINE.
LINE AT 19 AUG.
Scale - 1:1,000,000.

MAP 12.

CHAPTER TWO

The Capture of Antwerp

The Seine and the Somme

Before the end of August, the enemy had been forced to withdraw to the right bank of the Seine, practically throughout its length from Paris to the sea. The Commander-in-Chief's intention was now to destroy all the enemy forces in the Pas de Calais and Flanders and to capture the port of Antwerp.

The Second British Army was ordered to cross the Seine and establish itself in the area Arras—Amiens, regardless of the progress of the forces on its flanks. 30 Corps was given the task of driving on to Amiens and thus began the first of those operations in which it was to fight a lone battle, with its leading troops stretched out far ahead of the flanking formations.

By 24 August, reconnaissance parties of 43 Div had reached the Vernon area, where the Americans were holding the left bank of the Seine and it was planned that 43 Div should make an assault crossing of the river at this point. Early in the evening of 25 August, the leading troops of 43 Div crossed the river, under cover of a smoke screen put down on the opposite bank by their artillery. By 2100 hrs, four companies of 129 Inf Brigade were established on the eastern bank and opposition so far had not been strong. The bridgehead was extended on 26 August and by last light, in the face of intermittent sniping, a Class 9 bridge had been built across the river. By now the best part of 129 and 214 Inf Brigades had got across and one squadron of 8 Armd Brigade tanks was ferried across during the night. Approximately 200 prisoners had been captured during the day.

On 27 August, the enemy staged two counter attacks against the bridgehead and although both these were repulsed, a certain amount of interference was experienced troughout the day from enemy artillery and mortars, including a direct hit at midday on the bridge itself. But these incidents did not deter 43 Div from enlarging its bridgehead; at 1930 hrs that night its Class 40 bridge was completed and the remaining tanks of 8 Armd Brigade began to cross.

Meanwhile the forces to exploit this river crossing were being marshalled. 11 Armd Div was moving up from Laigle and 50 (N) Div had already arrived in the area southwest of Vernon. Guards Armd Div was also placed under command of 30 Corps and was ordered to move to Laigle. By 28 August, 43 Div had developed a firm bridgehead and the leading troops of 11 Armd Div started to cross the river.

The race to Amiens began on 29 August. By their successful crossing of the Seine, 43 Div had raised the starting gate and the Corps Commander now planned to advance with two armoured brigades up. 8 Armd Brigade right, 29 Armd Brigade left, both under command 11 Armd Div. 50 (N) Div were to follow up and Guards Armd Div would be committed as soon as it arrived.

The first day's advance went well and 1,000 prisoners were taken. Against organised restistance by small bodies of infantry and anti-tank guns, 29 Armd Brigade advanced nearly twenty miles on the left and by last light had reached Mainneville. Progress on the right was slower and 8 Armd Brigade had been unable to gain the outskirts of Gisors. The Corps Commander ordered the left column to keep up its northern advance even if the right could not get forward.

The next day, 8 Armd Brigade managed to enter Gisors about noon and passed on to Beauvais that afternoon. On the left, progress had been sustained and a further forty miles was covered by the advancing armour; by nightfall, 29 Armd Brigade had passed three miles beyond Crèvecour le Grande, and were only fifteen miles from Amiens. Another 1,000 prisoners had been taken and it was clear that the enemy's timetable for his withdrawal to the Somme had been completely upset by our amoured thrust.

Guards Armd Div which had started to cross the Seine at 1945 hrs on 29 August, was directed to advance on the right flank and by nightfall on 30 August was preparing to pass through 8 Armd Brigade in the Beauvais area.

MAP 13

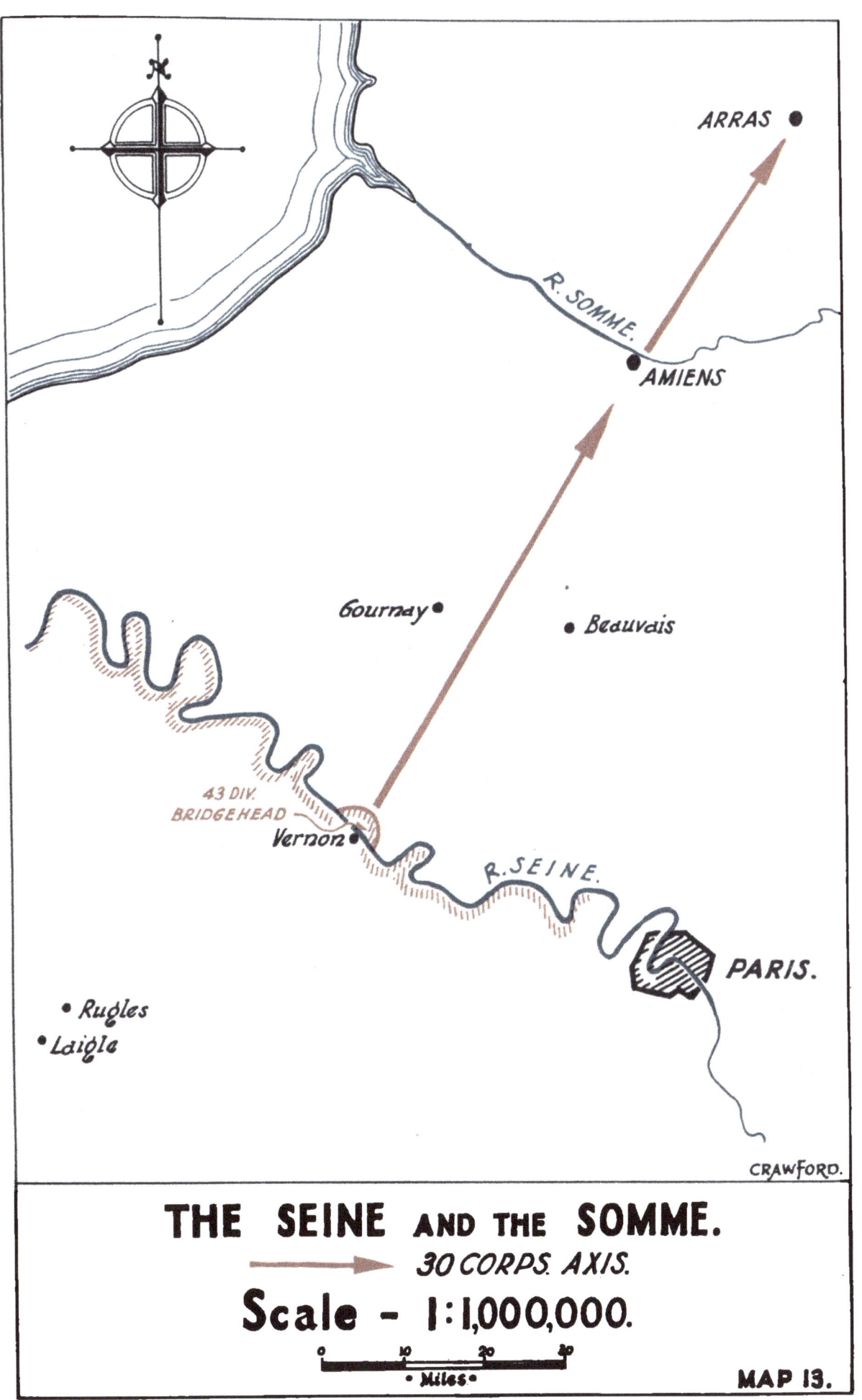

Then came the dramatic rush through the night by 11 Armd Div. Denying even a moment's respite to the harassed enemy, the leading armour did not leaguer for the night 30/31 August but pushed on for Amiens. It was rewarded for its dashing effort by two prizes. Firstly, it entered Amiens at 0645 hrs and took the main bridge into the town intact; secondly, it captured General Eberach, the Commander of 5 Pz and 7 Armies, together with his tactical headquarters. By 1700 hrs, all resistance in the town had ended and some 3,000 prisoners had been taken. The fact that these prisoners came from nearly one hundred different units shows the extent of chaos which had been caused to the enemy by our surprise capture of Amiens. Meanwhile Guards Armd Div, which had passed through 8 Armd Brigade early in the morning in the Beauvais area, had made astonishing progress on the right flank. Advancing almost unopposed, its leading regiments had reached the Somme east of Amiens and had captured two bridges intact. By nightfall on this memorable last day of August, both armoured divisions had crossed the Somme, 11 Armd Div protecting the northern outskirts of Amiens and the Guards holding the Amiens—Albert road; 8 Armd Brigade and the leading brigade of 50 (N) Div were also moving up to the Amiens area.

Since breaking out from the Seine bridgehead three days earlier, 140 miles had been covered, crossings had been gained over the Somme, and three divisions and an armoured brigade were now marshalled by the Corps ready to press on northwards.

The Advance to Antwerp and Brussels (Maps 14 and 15)

On 1 September, with Antwerp still the main Corps objective, both armoured divisions were directed from Amiens towards Arras, while 8 Armd Brigade was ordered to capture Doullens and then protect the Corps left flank. All objectives for the day were once again secured.

On the right, Guards Armd Div encountered initially stubborn resistance in the Albert area but shortly after midday its leading troops had entered Arras and had overrun the headquarters of the hastily formed enemy 'Somme' Corps, capturing its Commander and his staff. By nightfall its armoured cars had reached Lens and an armoured regiment had entered Douai; its armoured Brigade was positioned on the high ground north of Arras and its infantry Brigade was in the southern outskirts of the town. More than 2,500 prisoners had been captured during the day. In the centre, 11 Armd Div had encountered little opposition except from isolated pockets of the enemy and by 1600 hrs had gained its objectives to the north of Arras, and patrols were sent to Doullens and St Pol. More than 500 prisoners including the Commander of the enemy AA Somme Command and his headquarters had been captured. On the left, 8 Armd Brigade after some fierce fighting had captured Doullens and at last light was consolidating on its northern outskirts.

Progress on 2 September was slow; in marked contrast to the rapid advances of the preceding few days. Although the armoured divisions had reached the general line Carvin—Douai early in the day, Second Army ordered a "stand fast" so that an operation by airborne forces might be launched to seize the bridge at Tournai. (In fact, Tournai was occupied and the bridge was seized intact on this day by XIX US Corps.) At 2200 hours the projected airborne operation was cancelled and plans were made for the Corps advance into Belgium to be resumed again at first light.

The next day saw striking advances, averaging 65 miles, made by both armoured divisions. On the left, 11 Armd Div was at first considerably hampered by enemy armed with 88 mm guns, withdrawing eastwards from the Lille area. 50 (N) Div was therefore ordered to take up positions screening the exits from Lille, and thus prevent the enemy from interfering with the advance of our armour. Once having got clear of this opposition, 11 Armd Div moved fast and arrived by last light in the area of Alost. Meanwhile on the right axis the advance of the Guards went very smoothly. Crossing the American-held bridge at Tournai, it entered Belgium about 0900 hrs and just before last light its leading elements entered Brussels, where they were received with enthusiasm by the inhabitants. By 2200 hrs both its brigades had entered the city.

During the afternoon of 4 September, 11 Armd Div entered Antwerp and penetrated against sporadic resistance to the dock area. Thus the main Army Group objective had been secured by 30 Corps. Guards Armd Div pushed out a regimental group to Louvain, where it seized crossings over the Dyle, a river familiar to those who had fought in Europe in 1940. 50 (N) Div protecting the rear left flank entered

MAP 14

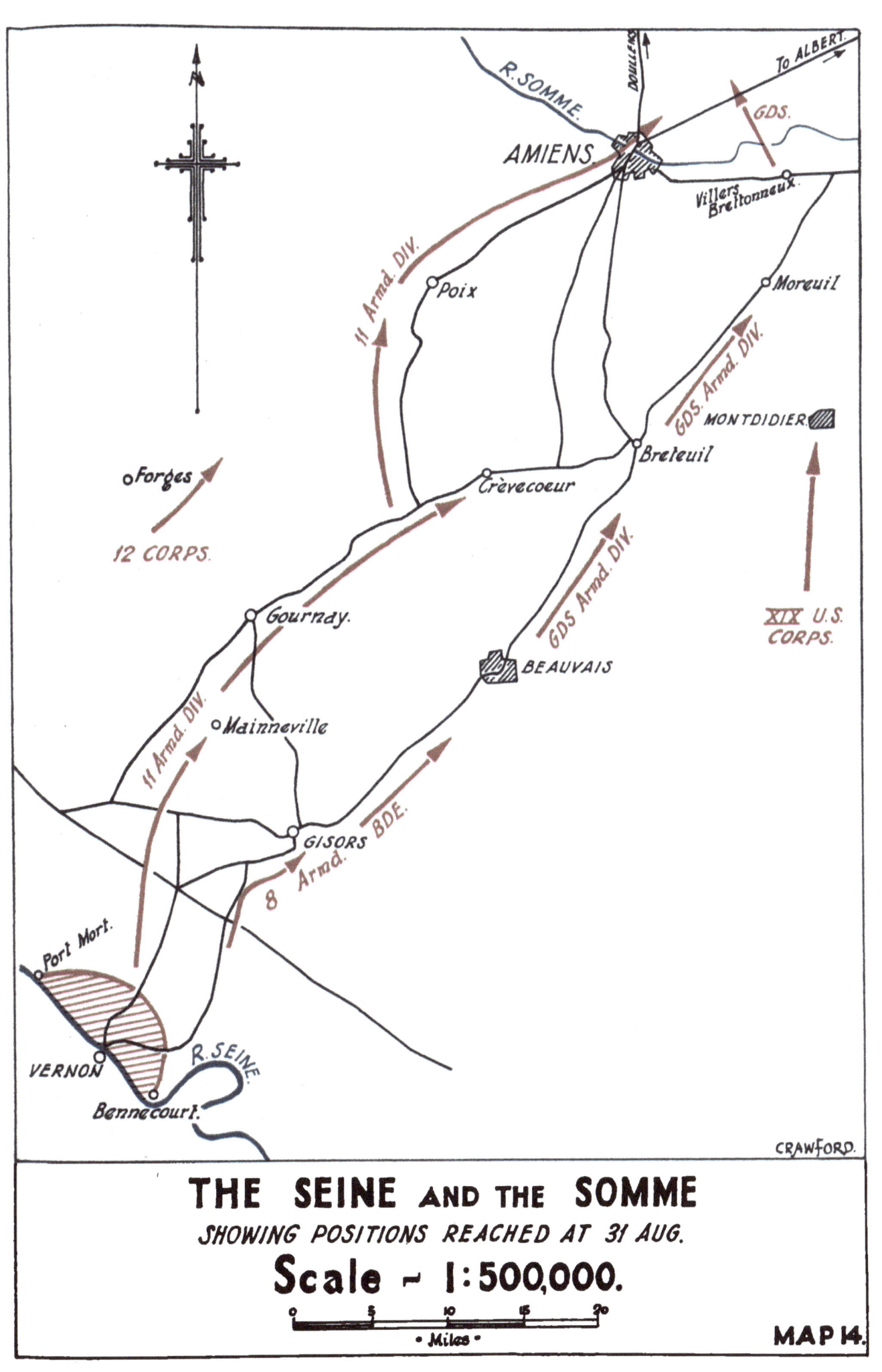

THE SEINE AND THE SOMME
SHOWING POSITIONS REACHED AT 31 AUG.
Scale ~ 1:500,000.

MAP 14.

MAP 15

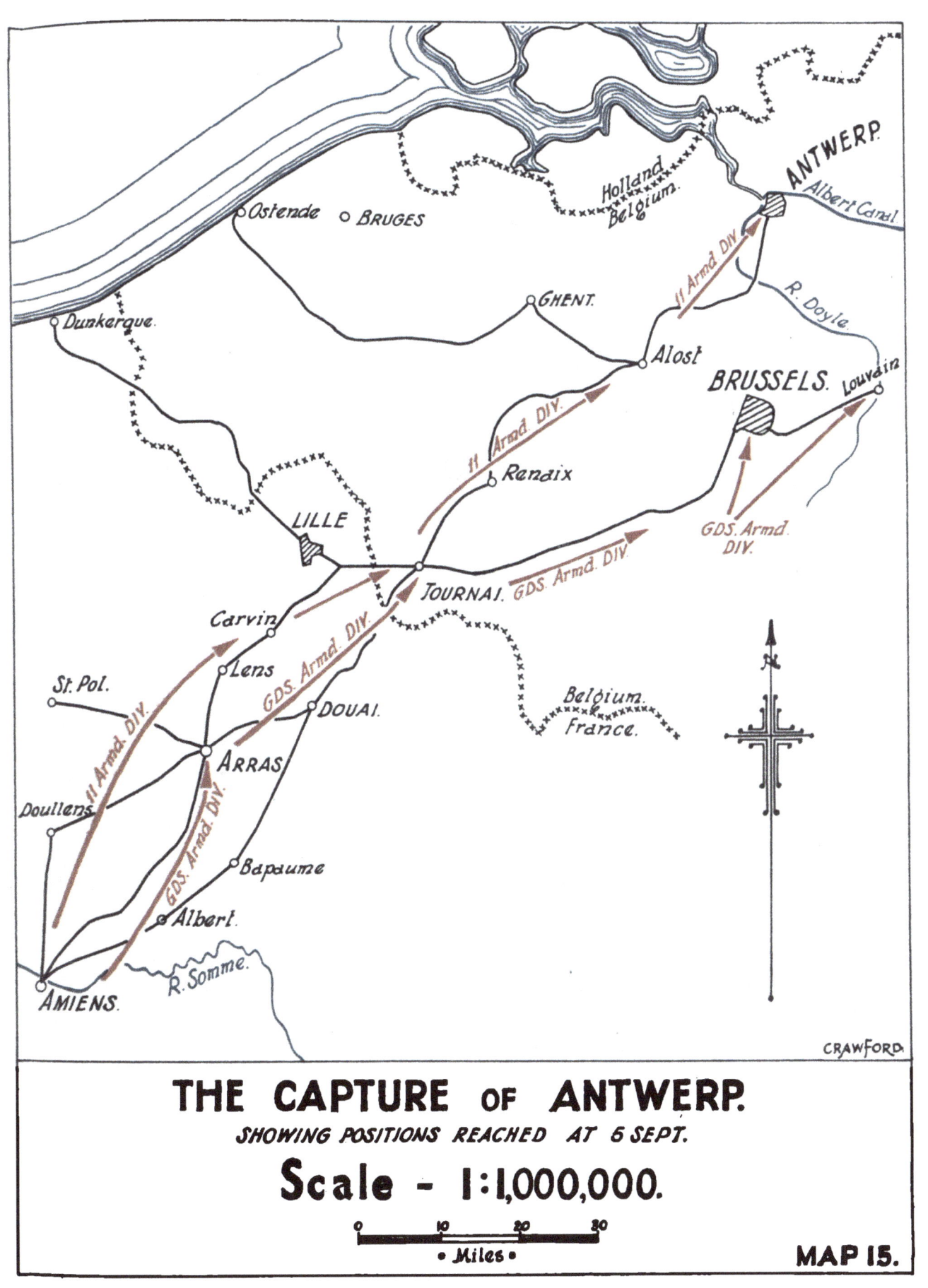

THE CAPTURE OF ANTWERP.
SHOWING POSITIONS REACHED AT 5 SEPT.
Scale - 1:1,000,000.

MAP 15.

Renaix and sent an Infantry Brigade up to protect the exits from Brussels. About midday on 4 September, Main Corps HQ threaded its way slowly through the cheering crowds in Brussels and leaguered in the grounds of the Chateau Royale at Laeken, just north of the city.

11 Armd Div spent 5 September in clearing Antwerp, where it was found that all the bridges across the Albert Canal were blown. The docks, however, were not severely damaged and there was every prospect of them being put readily into working order. 3,000 prisoners were collected this day from Antwerp alone. Guards Armd Div mopped up the area east of Brussels, particularly around Evère airfield which had been occupied under shell fire the previous day by 662 A.O.P. Squadron.

In less than two weeks, 30 Corps had forced crossings over the two great river obstacles, the Seine and the Somme. By its striking advance of some 250 miles, averaging more than 40 miles a day, it had secured the vital port of Antwerp and it had liberated the capital city of Belgium. The enemy defences had been overrun and disorganised; 20,000 enemy had been taken prisoner.

Crossing the Canals (Map 16)

September 6 was devoted to establishing bridgeheads across the Albert Canal. On the right, Guards Armd Div advanced from Louvain and managed to get a footing over a half demolished bridge at Beeringen and very quickly started to build another bridge alongside it. In the Antwerp area, one battalion of 11 Armd Div forced a crossing immediately north of the town, but very heavy mortaring and shelling delayed the start of bridging.

The Guards completed their bridge at Beeringen at midnight 6/7 September and by midday 7 September, one armoured battle group had crossed the canal and taken Helchteren. The armoured recce regiment was then swung northwards and engaged in a fierce battle on the road to Hechtel, which was strongly held by enemy paratroops. It was estimated that the Guards Armd Div killed 500 enemy and took 300 prisoners that day. Meanwhile at Antwerp all efforts to complete the 11 Armd Div bridge proved unsuccessful. It was decided at this point that 12 Corps, which had now arrived, should take over the Antwerp flank and that 11 Armd Div, thus freed from its commitments there, should be directed to the right flank of 30 Corps.

By now 50 (N) Div, which still had brigades in Brussels and Antwerp, had been brought up to the canal on the left of Guards Armd Div and, on 8 September, it forced two crossings south of Gheel. Simultaneously, two regiments of 8 Armd Brigade were put across the Beeringen bridge with the object of linking up with 50 (N) Div in the Gheel area. At this stage the enemy, who was obviously endeavouring to hold our advance on the line of the canal, committed considerable reinforcements, most of which were paratroops. The two battalions of 50 (N) Div which had crossed the canal were called upon to repulse no less than four counter-attacks during the afternoon and the 8 Armd Brigade regiments were stubbornly opposed in the woods about two miles northwest of Beeringen. Particularly heavy fighting was also experienced by the Guards Armd Div round Hechtel crossroads, where the resistance was exceptionally bitter.

Throughout 9 September the increase in enemy strength against the Corps became more and more apparent. There were now sixteen enemy battalions and about fifty tanks deployed between the Escaut and the Albert canals. It appeared that the enemy's immediate plan was to liquidate the Gheel bridgehead and then deal with Beeringen later. Consequently the main force of his attacks fell upon 50 (N) Div whose bridgeheads were still perilously narrow. But the Beeringen bridges did not escape attention, for a party of forty picked men were briefed by the notorious parachutist van der Heydte to infiltrate through our bridgehead there and blow up the bridges. They failed in their mission but during the night they wrought heavy destruction amid a leaguer of echelon vehicles. Fighting continued most bitterly at Hechtel, where the crossroads had become a bloody no-man's-land with Hubner's fanatical battle group holding one side and the Guards opposing them at point blank range on the other.

10 September will always be notable for the dramatic capture of "Joe's Bridge" by the Guards Armd Div. After a heavy day's fighting, a small party of Irish Guards succeeded in reaching the Escaut canal and, knocking out its covering force of six 88 mm guns, captured this bridge intact. "Joe's Bridge" has no other name; it lies just west of Neerpelt and is a gateway into Holland. Meanwhile heavy fighting continued right along the Corps front. On the right flank, where 11 Armd Div had now been directed, a fierce battle took place in the

Helchteren area resulting in the death of 200 enemy and the capture of over 450 prisoners. In the centre, the Guards were still heavily engaged around Hechtel. On the left flank, 50 (N) Div, which now had two brigades across the canal, repulsed several counter attacks and captured Gheel with some 700 prisoners.

There then followed a period of consolidation and re-grouping before the dash into Holland, commenced on 17 September. The bridgehead over the Escaut canal was strengthened first by infantry and tanks of Guards Armd Div and later by 231 Inf Brigade of 50 (N) Div. 11 Armd Div pressed up to the canal on the Corps right flank. In order that 50 (N) Div should be available to advance with 30 Corps in the forthcoming operation, 12 Corps was ordered to start taking over the Gheel bridgehead on 12 September. On the following day, 43 Div was ordered to join 30 Corps from the River Seine, where it had remained after its crossing at Vernon. On the 16 September, 11 Armd Div passed to command 8 Corps, which had now arrived on the right flank.

Within fourteen days, the Corps had traversed the width of Belgium — rarely in history can this much-contested battle ground have been so quickly liberated. In addition that classic water obstacle, the Albert Canal, had been stormed and crossed. The determined efforts of the enemy to halt the Corps first on this line and then on the Meuse — Escaut Canal had been frustrated. With firm bridgeheads established across these canals, the stage was set for another dash northwards by 30 Corps; this time to Holland and the Rhine.

MAP 16

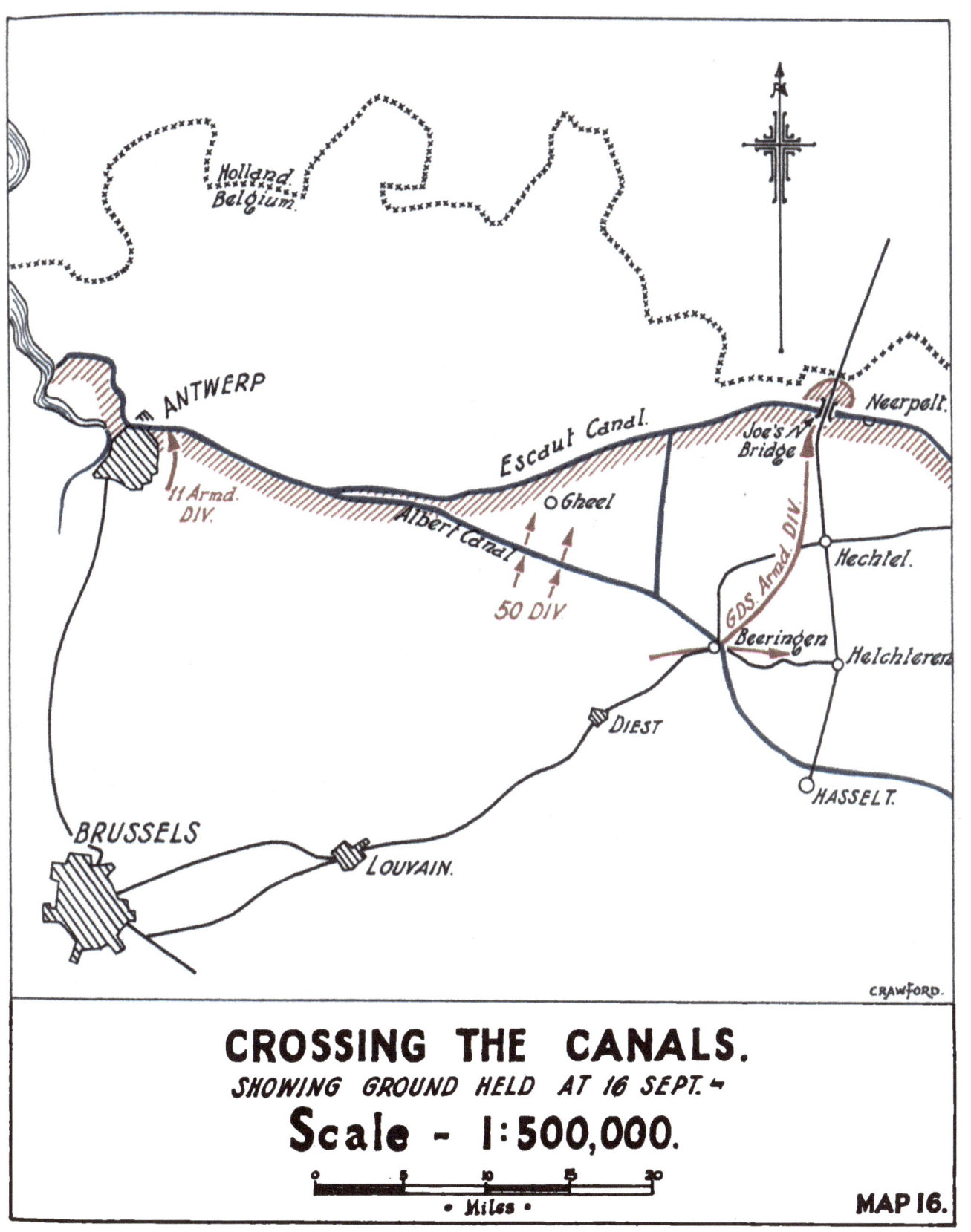

CROSSING THE CANALS.
SHOWING GROUND HELD AT 16 SEPT.
Scale - 1:500,000.

MAP 16.

CHAPTER THREE

The Advance to Arnhem

From the Escaut to the Waal (Maps 17 and 18)

As soon as 30 Corps had gained its small bridgehead across the Meuse—Escaut canal, it learned of the ambitious attempt to be made to thrust northwards to the Zuider Zee. Second Army, with airborne forces under command, was to position itself in the general area Grave—Nijmegen—Arnhem and to dominate toe country to the north, thereby cutting off communications between Germany and the Low Countries.

30 Corps * was to advance on one main axis and secure the area Nunspeet—Arnhem; 8 Corps and 12 Corps were to protect the right and left flanks respectively. The airborne troops * were to capture intact the river crossings and to facilitate the advance of 30 Corps by seizing nodal points on its axis (Map 17). This joint operation was known as operation Market Garden; the part to be carried out by 30 Corps being known as operation Garden.

It was estimated that the enemy strength which would immediately oppose the breakout of the Corps was approximately six infantry battalions and 20 AFVs. Though, if the operation were successful, it was appreciated that all the resources of the enemy 15 Army in Holland might be turned against the Corps.

The Corps Commander decided that the Guards Armd Div should make the breakout and lead the advance, followed by 43 Div and 50 Div, in that order. The assembling and marshalling of forces before the operation required careful organisation. It had to be so flexible

---

* Order of Battle at Appendix "B".

that the Corps Commander could call forward any body of troops he required, once the Guards Armd Div had broken through, and thus no fixed order of march for the 20,000 vehicles in the Corps could be prescribed. It was also clear that the breakout would be difficult as, not only was the bridgehead small, but the country north of Joe's Bridge was heavily wooded and very marshy, making it impossible for the armour to move off the road. Bearing this in view, the Corps Commander directed that the breakout should be supported by a very intense artillery programme and by a heavy Typhoon bombardment.

On the morning of D Day, 17 September 1944, Second Army confirmed that operation Market Garden would take place that day and, at 1230 hrs, the Corps Commander at his Recce HQ overlooking the Meuse—Escaut canal received a signal that the airborne forces had left their bases in the UK. Shortly afterwards the leading planes of the airborne lift, the largest yet attempted in any operation, were sighted. The Corps Commander thereupon ordered Z hour, the time at which the Guards would attack, to be 1435 hrs. Shortly after 1400 hrs, some 300 guns of the Corps artillery opened up a narrow rolling barrage along the axis and the first squadron of R. P. Typhoons swooped down on the road to Valkenswaard. No less than seven squadrons, at five minute intervals, then continued to attack every known enemy locality ahead of the leading troops. It was a magnificent example of air support in the tactical battle.

The assault was led by an Irish Guards group of tanks and infantry. Stiff opposition was encountered from the start from two Para Bns and two bns of 9 SS Div, and by 1500 hrs the Guards were halted just north of the Dutch frontier. To overcome this temporary check, fresh waves of Typhoons were committed and part of the artillery barrage was fired again; this had the desired effect and by last light the Guards had reached Valkenswaard. 231 Inf Brigade moving up behind the Guards Armd Div cleared the woods on either side of the main axis.

Meanwhile the airborne landings had been most successful and had met only limited opposition. The bridge at Grave was seized intact by 82 US Airborne Div, whilst the bridges at Nijmegen and Arnhem were known to be intact but were not in our hands. Further, 101 US Airborne Div was firmly established on the Corps axis at Son, and near St Oedenrode and Veghel. The bridge over the canal at Son, however, was blown.

MAP 17

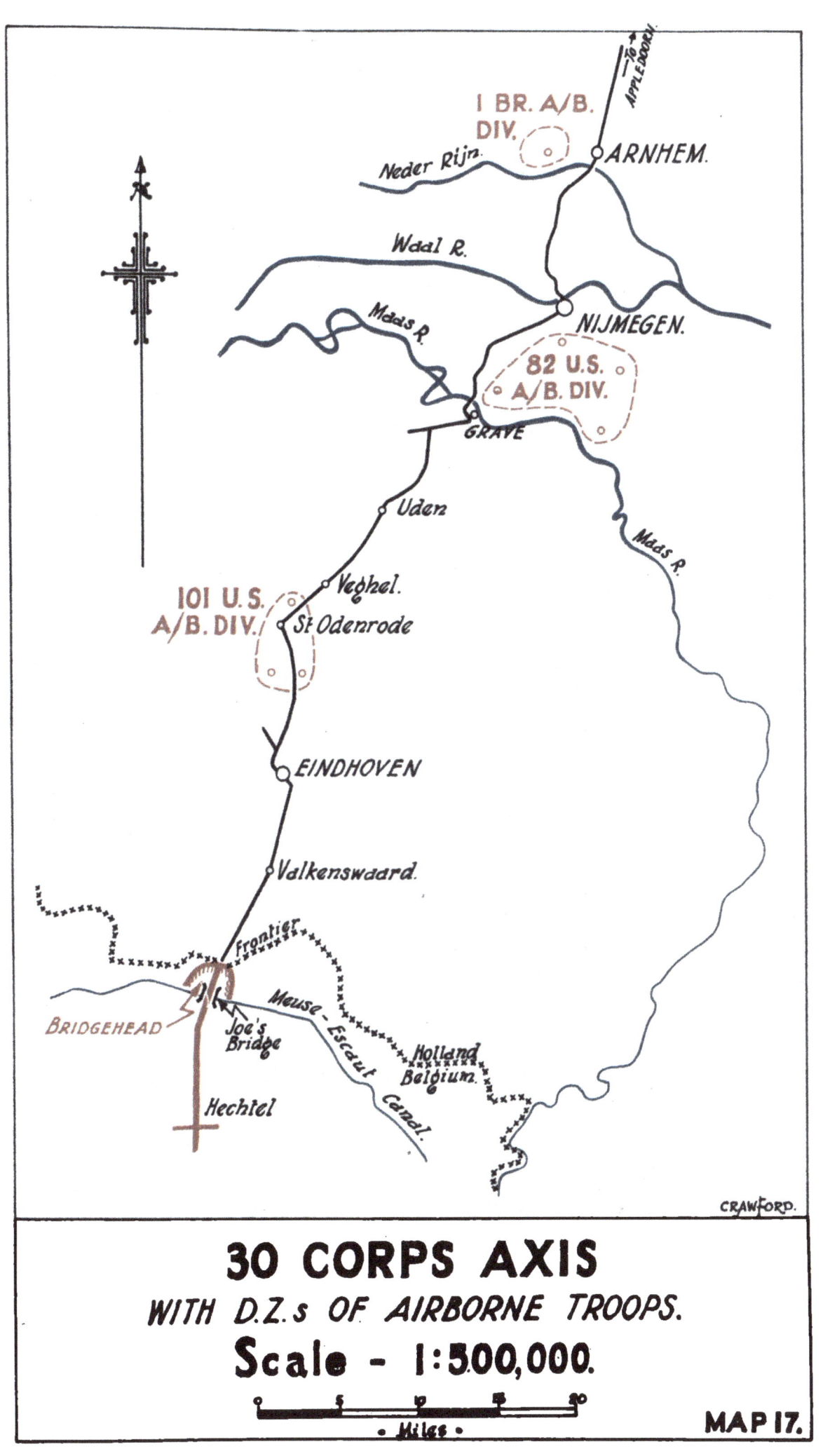

30 CORPS AXIS
WITH D.Z.s OF AIRBORNE TROOPS.
Scale – 1:500,000.

MAP 17.

MAP 18

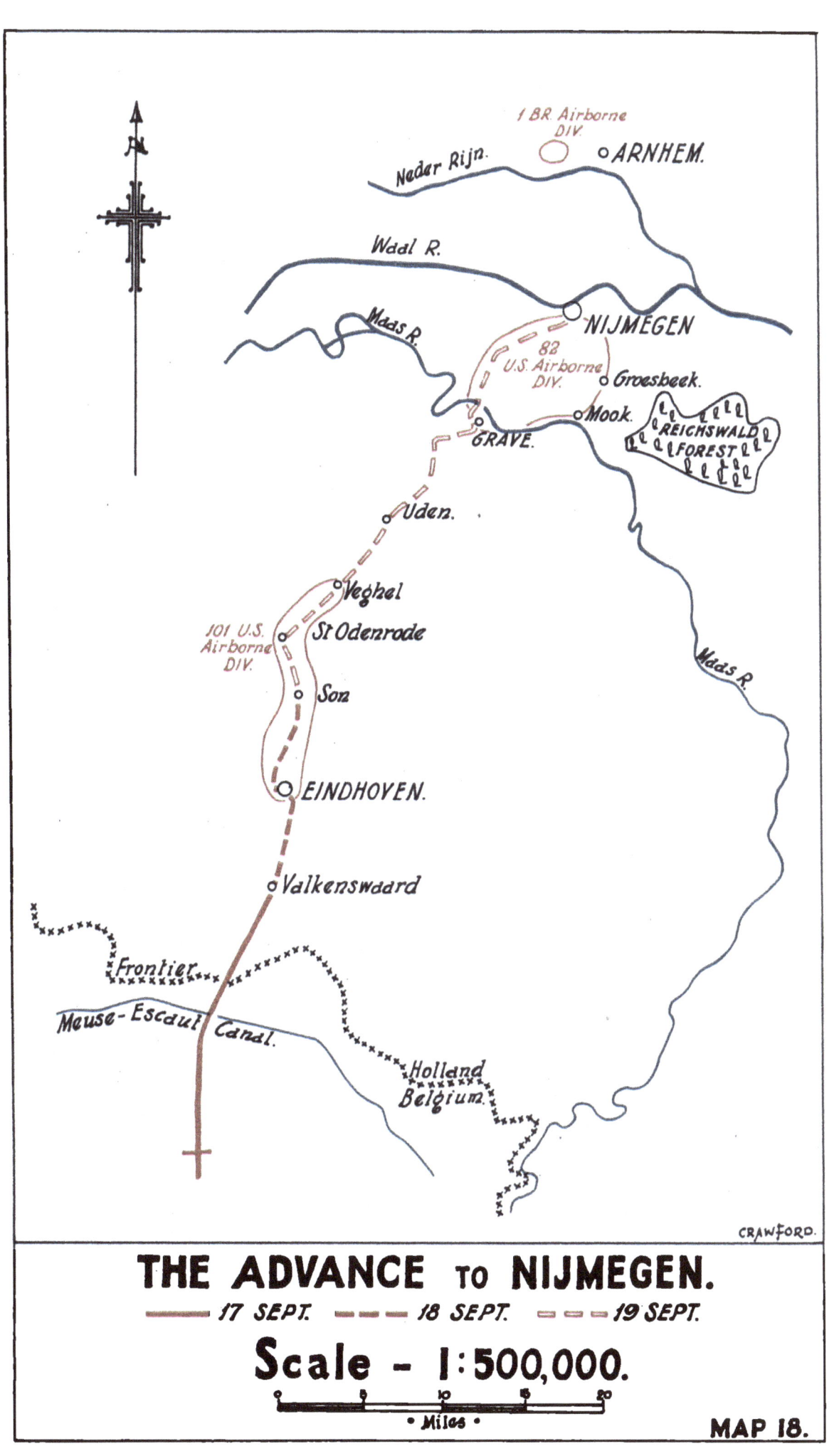

The following day, 18 September, the Guards Armd Div continued to meet strong opposition but by nightfall had linked up with 101 US Div at Eindhoven and that night rapidly replaced the blown bridge at Son. Throughout the day, the enemy attacked the Corps bridgehead over the Meuse—Escaut canal, but all their attacks were successfully repelled by 50 Div *. In the Nijmegen area, 82 US Airborne Div penetrated within 300 yards of the Waal bridge and were firmly established on the high ground south of the town. The situation at Arnhem was obscure but it was thought that 1 British Airborne Div was established to the west of the town and that 1 Para Brigade was holding the north end of Arnhem bridge.

Early on 19 September, leading troops of Guards Armd Div crossed the Son bridge and passed unopposed up the Corps axis, crossing the river Meuse by Grave bridge during the morning. Later in the day, in conjunction with troops of 82 US Airborne Div, they made an unsuccessful attempt to rush the Waal bridge at Nijmegen. This bridge was bitterly defended by elements of 9 SS Div, who were holding well defended positions commanding all its approaches. At Arnhem, the position of 1 Para Brigade on the north end of the bridge was gradually becoming less secure. The re-supply arrangements for the 1 Br Airborne Div had become difficult owing to the smallness of the perimeter occupied and it was known that the Div was becoming short of ammunition and supplies. It was also on 19 September, at 1900 hrs, that the enemy made the first of his efforts to cut the main Corps axis. Launching a tank attack, well supported by 88 mm guns, he attempted to re-capture the bridge at Son but was repulsed by 44 RTR and American Airborne troops. This action, together with the enemy bombing of Eindhoven, that night, delayed the advance of Main Corps HQ which had left Hechtel at 1740 hrs, 19 September, and did not succed in reaching its destination, Malden, until more than 24 hrs later. The Corps Commander's Recce HQ, however, had been established, without incident, at Malden before Main HQ left Hechtel and had made contact with the Commander of the Airborne Corps in Nijmegen. From then onwards, the two Corps Commanders worked in very close touch.

The crossing of the Waal (Map 19)

At this point two paramount tasks faced the Corps: to capture the Nijmegen bridge intact (or to force an assault crossing of the river

---

* In order to relieve 30 Corps of the responsibility for safeguarding the bridgehead area, 50 Div passed temporarily under command of 8 Corps. This was the first time that 50 Div had left operational command of 30 Corps since August 1943.

Waal) and to relieve the 1 Br Airborne Div. The two Corps Commanders therefore decided early on the 20 September that the Guards and 82 US Airborne Div should jointly clear the built-up area south of Nijmegen road bridge and that 504 US Para Inf Regt should undertake an assault crossing of the R. Waal west of Nijmegen. The advance through Nijmegen commenced at first light and proceeded from house to house throughout the day. At 1500 hrs, supported by fire from British and American guns and tanks of the Irish Guards, the paratroops launched their assault boats into the swift flowing Waal and set off on their hazardous daylight crossing of the great river, in the face of intense enemy fire. Only a few of the leading waves reached the far bank, some in boats and some swimming; these few gallant survivors succeeded in forming a precarious bridgehead 100 yards deep. Follow-up waves joined them and by 1800 hrs the small force started to move eastwards towards the Nijmegen bridges. Shortly afterwards, the Grenadier Guards received a report that the American flag could be seen on the far side of the road bridge *.

This bridge is approximately 700 yards long and has an embankment of equal length on the far side, which makes it impossible for tracked vehicles to leave the road for a distance of almost a mile. The bridge was known to be prepared for demolition and might be blown at any time. Nevertheless the Guards decided that they would attempt to rush the bridge and join the Americans on the North bank.

A troop of tanks of 2 Armd Bn, Grenadier Guards was accordingly ordered to dash across the bridge. Forming up on the southern approach, the troop was immediately engaged by heavy fire from 88 mm guns firing from the opposite bank and from an SP anti-tank gun shooting directly across the bridge. These guns were engaged by the Grenadiers' tanks which then managed to cross the bridge under withering fire, especially from enemy small arms and bazookas which were sited in the girders of the bridge itself. On reaching the far side of the bridge, they knocked out the SP gun which was firing down the road and then continued to advance and engage the enemy at close quarters until they made contact with the Americans about one mile north of the river.

Immediately behind this leading troop of tanks, an RE officer crossed the bridge to ensure that the demolition charges were removed

---

* This subsequently turned out to have been placed on the railway bridge some distance to the west of the road bridge.

MAP 19

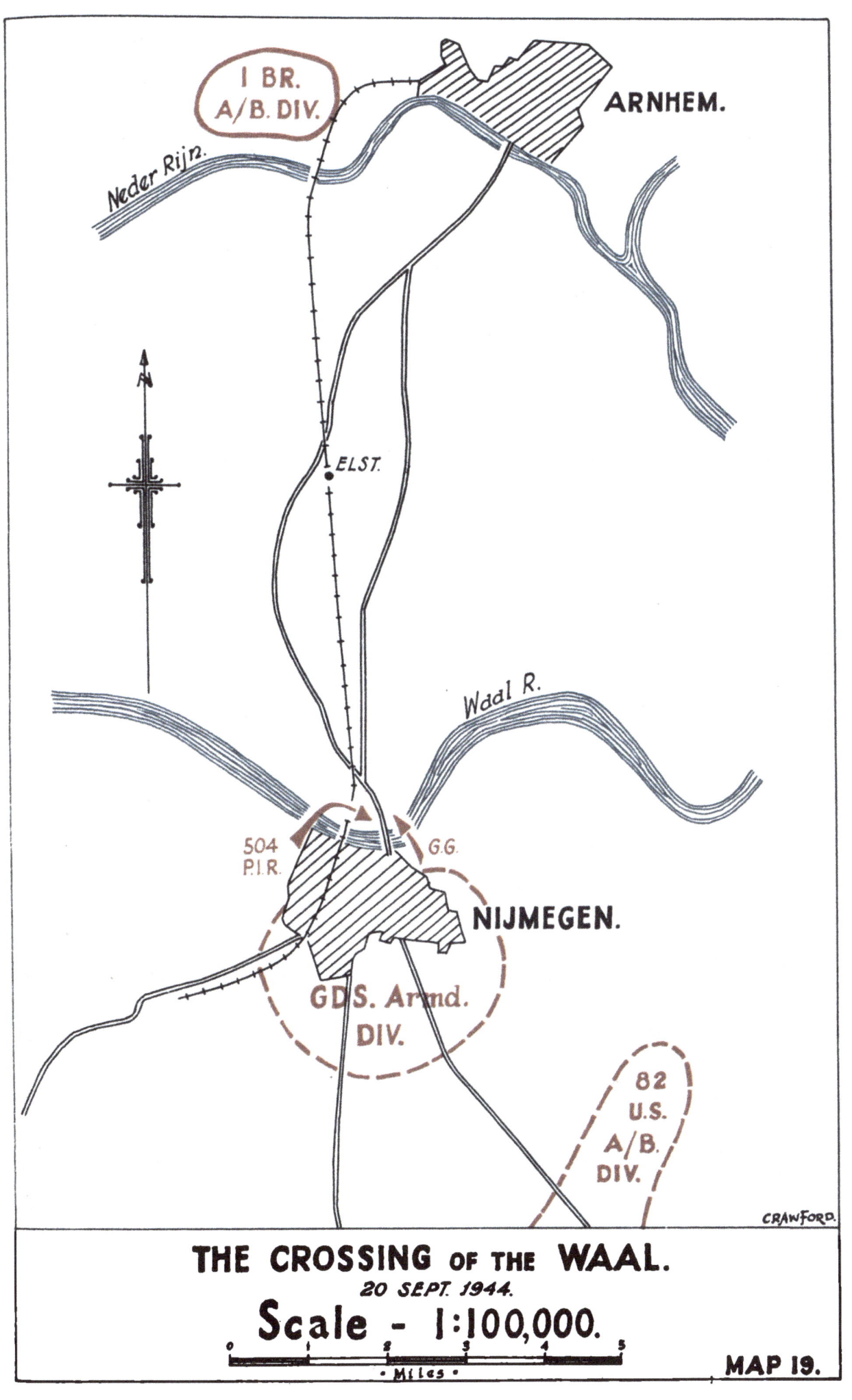

or rendered inoperative. The bridge was still infested with Germans, some of whom were shooting down from the girders, but, with great courage, the RE officer managed to cut the demolition wires and to locate the explosive chamber.

Tanks and Infantry of the Guards Armd Div then crossed and by last light a firm bridgehead had been established. Thus by a brilliant British-American action, one of the most important bridges in Europe had been captured intact, in the face of desperate resistance by some of the most fanatical elements of the enemy.

The fighting on "The Island" (Maps 20 and 21)

But in front, on the flanks and in the rear, all was not well. In the Arnhem area, the 1 Br Airborne Div was now holding only a small perimeter to the west of the town and Arnhem itself was entirely in the hands of the enemy. A message was also received from the Division that its resources were stretched to the uttermost and that relief was vital within the next 48 hours. On the right flank, the enemy counterattacked the 82 US Airborne Div in the Groesbeek and Mook areas and was reported to be massing reserves in the Reichswald Forest*. To the right rear, 8 Corps had not yet succeeded in reaching the Dutch frontier; while on the left, 12 Corps was still southwest of Eindhoven (Map 20). Furthermore, the enemy had made another attempt during the day to cut the Corps axis, in the vicinity of Son—St Oedenrode. This attack was repulsed but it succeeded in delaying the flow of traffic for three important hours.

Nevertheless, the capture of Nijmegen bridge had brought the Corps very much nearer to its immediate goal — the relief of the 1 Br Airborne Div at Arnhem. On 21 September, Guards Armd Div was ordered to advance at maximum speed to Arnhem and to make contact at all costs with the airborne troops. However, the country on "the Island" between the rivers Nederrijn and Waal was not suitable for tanks and it was therefore imperative to bring forward more infantry. By this time, 130 Inf Brigade of 43 Div had already arrived to take over Nijmegen and to secure the railway bridge. But this was not enough. So the Corps Commander ordered the remainder of 43 Div forward and directed them to reinforce the western flank of the Guards thrust to Arnhem. Throughout 21 September, the Irish Guards group

---

* Fighting on this right flank with the Americans were the Sherwood Rangers Yeomanry of the 8 Armd Brigade, who were thus the first British fighting troops to enter Germany. They were shortly reinforced by a group of the Coldstream Guards.

fought stubbornly but by now the enemy had strongly reinforced his troops on "the Island", especially with SP and Anti-tank guns. He had in fact formed a screen in the area of Ressen station, which proved impossible to penetrate. During the day about two thirds of the Polish Para Brigade were dropped north of Elst, with a view to crossing the Nederrijn to reinforce the 1 Br Airborne Div. (Map 21).

Ever since the first landing of the airborne troops, one of the difficulties confronting the Commanders had been the lack of information regarding the situation of 1 Br Airborne Div in the Arnhem area. Communications between this formation and the Airborne Corps had been most unsatisfactory throughout the operation. It was therefore extremely fortunate when, on the morning of 21 September the CRA of 1 Br Airborne Div was heard calling up on the Regimental net of 64 Med Regt RA. Identity was soon established and from that moment onwards invaluable artillery support was given to the airborne troops north of the Nederrijn by all the artillery of 30 Corps, which was within range. Originally most of this support was provided by 64 Med Regt RA and it was afterwards reported that the accurate and sustained fire provided by this regiment did much to assist 1 Br Airborne Div in holding its small perimeter west of Arnhem. This wireless link, which proved to be the only reliable means of communication, also became invaluable for the transmission of orders between the Airborne Div and its parent Corps.

The Corps Commander now decided to pass 43 Div through the left of Guards Armd Div. 43 Div was ordered to make contact with 1 Br Airborne Div and, if possible, to occupy the Arnhem bridge. Early on 22 September, patrols of HCR made a rush to the south bank of the Nederrijn and made contact with the Polish paracutists. Meanwhile 43 Div, after a hard day's fighting, successfully broke out of the Waal bridgehead. Thereupon 214 Inf Brigade, which had been waiting for just this opportunity, rushed a mobile column consisting of 5 DCLI and a squadron of 4/7 DG, with DUKWs laden with supplies for the Airborne Div, through Valburg and after an exciting journey during which five Tiger tanks joined the column they linked up with the Poles at Driel. The advance of 129 Inf Brigade on the road to Arnhem made little progress and by last light they were still south of Elst. An attempt was made that night to ferry reinforcements and supplies across

MAP 20

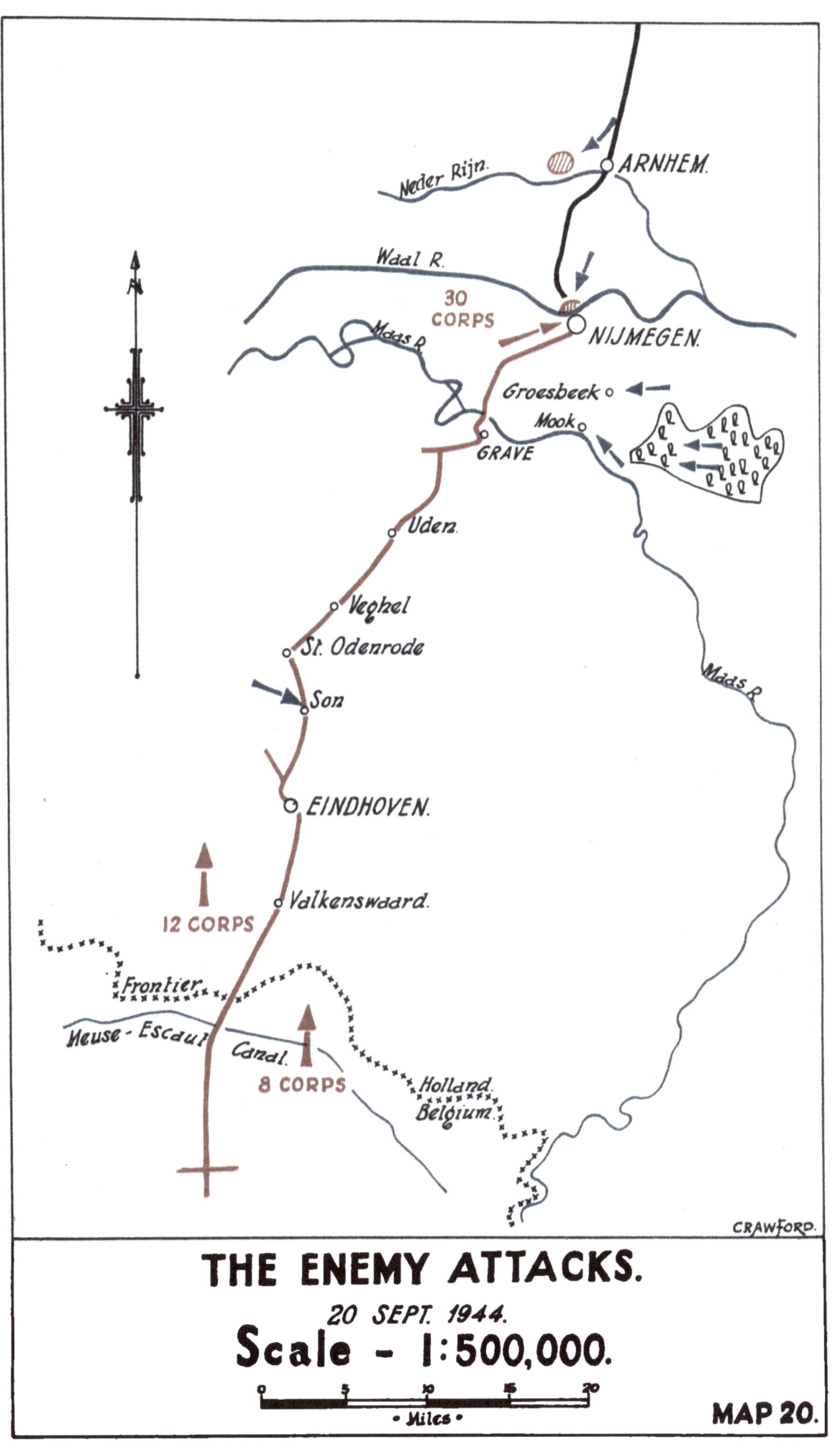

THE ENEMY ATTACKS.
20 SEPT. 1944.
Scale - 1:500,000.

MAP 20.

MAP 21

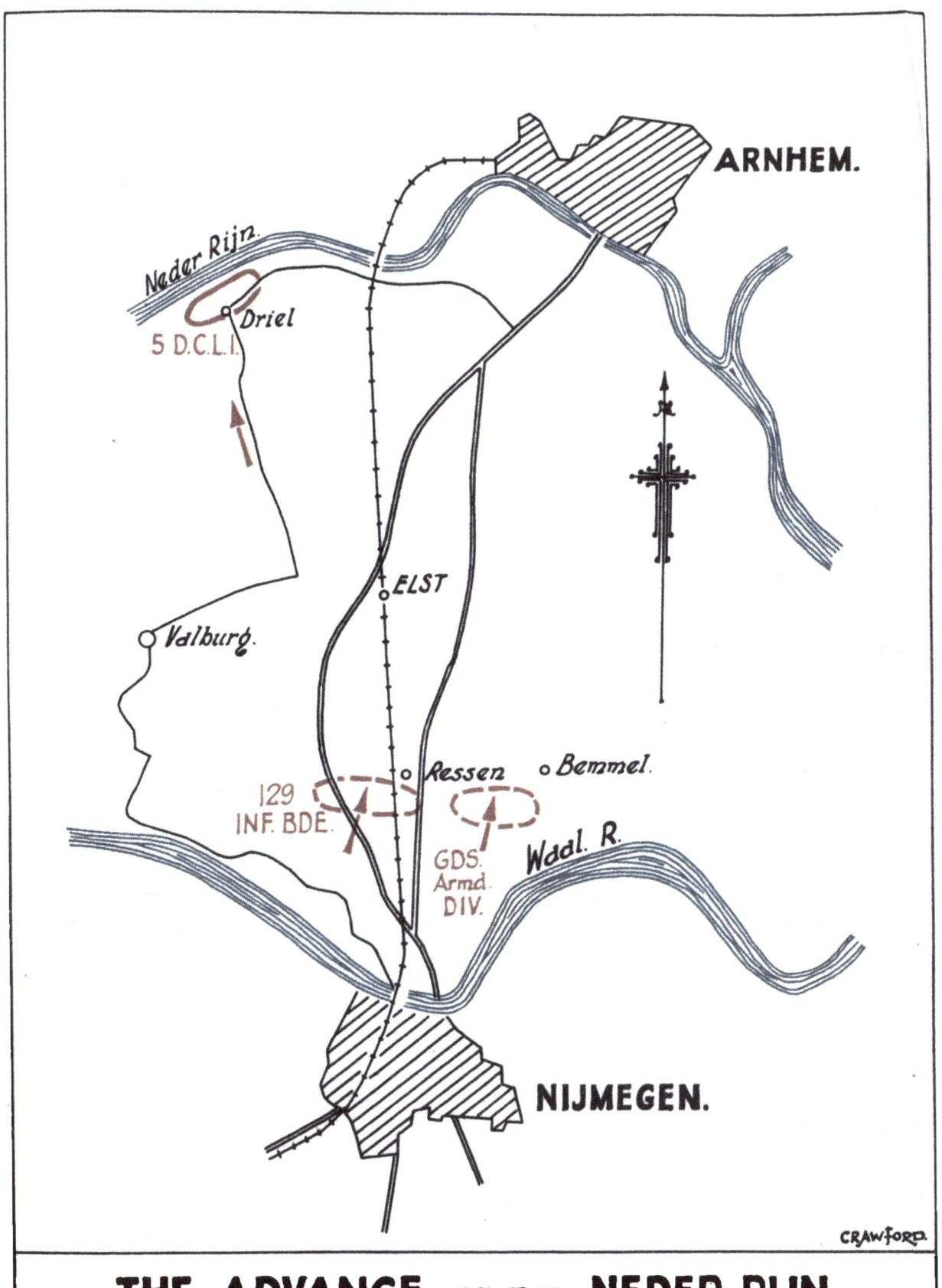

THE ADVANCE TO THE NEDER RIJN.
22 SEPT. 1944.
Scale – 1:100,000.

MAP 21.

to the airborne troops on the north of the river, but little got across because the banks proved too steep for DUKWs to use and the whole of the southern bank was under Spandau fire.

It was on this day, 22 September, that the enemy first succeeded in his efforts to cut the Corps axis. Attacking from the northwest with tanks, lorried infantry and SP guns, he breached the axis between Uden and Veghel. To meet this thrust the Corps Commander despatched 32 Guards Brigade from the Nijmegen area and by evening contact had been made south of Grave. But no decisive action took place that night and for 25 precious hours the supplies so vitally required to maintain the offensive were prevented from moving up the single Corps artery.

The 23 September was spent by 43 Div in strengthening and deepening the existing bridgehead so that a firm link with 1 Br Airborne Div could be achieved that night and 5 Dorsets were successfully pushed forward to join the DCLI on the south bank of the Nederrijn. Heavy fighting took place throughout the day in Elst and southwest of Bemmel. Unfortunately the enemy on the north bank of the river captured the important ferry west of Arnhem and this greatly hampered the despatch of reinforcements that evening. In spite of every effort, during the hours of darkness, only a few Polish paratroops were ferried across and all the boats containing stores were sunk by enemy machine-guns firing on fixed lines across the river.

On 24 September, elements of 6 Para Regt again cut the Corps axis south of Veghel. On "The Island", 43 Div continued very fierce house to house fighting and Guards Armd Div, which now had the leading brigade (69 Inf Brigade) of 50 Div under command, attempted unsuccessfully to capture Bemmel. The position of the airborne troops north of the river was still precarious but, in addition to very sustained artillery support, they were also supported throughout the day by an almost endless procession of Typhoons. During the night 4 Dorsets succeeded in sending 350 men with mortars and gunner OPs across the river. In addition some three tons of stores were ferried across.

The withdrawal from Arnhem

By 25 September preparations to establish a bridgehead in the area west of Arnhem had been put in hand by 43 Div. But that morning it was decided to withdraw 1 Br Airborne Div during the following night, 25/26 September. The small bridgehead had by now become virtually untenable owing to casualties and shortage of supplies. Furthermore there was little prospect of expanding the bridgehead as reinforcements could only be got over on a limited scale in assault boats under cover of darkness, across a stretch of river which was completely dominated both from northeast and northwest. Also, owing to the enemy operations against the Corps axis there was a shortage of assault boats and artillery ammunition.

While plans for the withdrawal were being made there was no decrease in the ferocity of the fighting on "The Island". The enemy were finally cleared from Elst by 43 Div and by dusk he had been pushed out of Bemmel by 50 Div, who had taken over this task from Guards Armd Div. The Corps main axis was still not cleared and no traffic had passed along it for 24 hours.

Throughout the night 25/26 September, 4 Dorsets operated to cover the withdrawal of 1 Br Airborne Div. A heavy artillery programme was fired to cover the withdrawal, all ammunition down to 25 rounds per gun being fired by the field guns of the Corps that night. By great gallantry and skill, 2,323 airborne troops were safely brought across the river but this had only been done at the cost of some 200 men of 4 Dorsets, who had ensured the success of the evacuation by their gallant fighting to widen the bridgehead.

Thus ended the audacious attempt to reach the Zuider Zee. Crossings had been captured over two of the three main rivers; bridges were secure over the Meuse and the Waal but the Nederrijn remained uncrossed. Second Army had thrust deep into German occupied Holland and had gained a footing on "The Island" which it was never to lose. In a period of ten days, the Corps had advanced over 60 miles and, in spite of determined enemy interference, had succeeded in marshalling more than 25,000 vehicles up the solitary Corps axis.

On 29 September, both the bridges at Nijmegen were temporarily put out of action. At 0500 hrs that morning, two parties of German swimmers in primitive diving equipment had placed explosive charges against the piers of the bridges. The damage to the railway bridge was serious and was never repaired; but in the road bridge a gap of only 80 feet was blown and this was successfully filled by Bailey bridging.

Unable to destroy the bridges by this means, the enemy then committed many of his reserves in determined efforts to recapture the bridges. On the night 1/2 October, he put in an attack with elements of 1 SS and 12 SS Divs against Groesbeek and almost immediately afterwards committed 9 Pz and 116 Pz Divs in attacks north of the Waal in the area of Elst. But all these attacks and those which followed were repulsed; if ground was lost it was quickly regained by counter attack and heavy losses were inflicted on the enemy. On one day alone 400 prisoners were captured and 90 dead were counted.

But it was not long before all enemy reserves were required elsewhere for the Americans had breached the Siegfried Line and were threatening Aachen. So the enemy was henceforth forced to adopt a defensive attitude on the Corps front and for a period activity was confined to patrols.

On 8 October, 12 Corps took over command of all troops on "The Island" and 30 Corps was left free to concentrate on the south-eastern front between the Waal and the Maas. Planning was now stated for an attack eastwards through the Reichswald, in which the major role was to be undertaken by 43 Div. Known as "Operation Wyvern", this attack was never staged but much preparatory work was put into its planning (this was to prove useful two and three months later when its successor, Operation Veritable, was being planned).

On 18 October, 30 Corps again took over "The Island". It was known at this time that the enemy, by blowing the dyke banks of the Nederrijn, could rapidly flood the whole area of "The Island" to a depth of several feet. Plans were therefore made to evacuate this area should it become necessary. In fact, no attempt to inundate "The Island" was made while 30 Corps was occupying it; it was, however, partially flooded later in the winter.

Towards the end of October reports were received that a number of 1 Br Airborne Div were still together north of the Nederrijn. Arrangements were therefore made by the Corps for their rescue and on the evening 22/23 October a strong force from 101 US Airborne Div with detachments of 30 Corps RE crossed the river. They succeeded in contacting the British Airborne Troops and by a most skilful operation, in the face of the enemy, they succeeded in bringing 138 men safely back across the Nederrijn. Another exceptionally audacious performance was staged on the 31 October by a six man patrol of 101 US Airborne Div. The patrol crossed the Nederrijn and, moving far into enemy territory, set up an OP in a house occupied by two Germans. The OP was manned throughout the day and then, as darkness fell, the Americans laid a "vehicle trap" on the main Arnhem — Utrecht road. Within a short time this yielded two trucks and sixteen prisoners. Together with the six prisoners who had been collected previously, the complete party was then marched southwards and, posing as a German platoon, successfully passed through the German held town of Renkum. They moved safely down to the river bank, capturing nine more prisoners on the way. A pre-arranged light signal brought boats from the opposite bank and all the prisoners and their captors were safely carried back to the US lines.

At the beginning of November plans were made for the relief of 30 Corps in the Nijmegen Sector by 2 Canadian Corps. 30 Corps were destined to take over part of the front from 9 US Army in the area of Geilenkirchen and would there become the right hand formation of 21 Army Group. Command of the Nijmegen Sector passed to the Canadians at 1200 hours on the 9 November and immediately afterwards Main Corps HQ moved to Beek, near Maastricht.

CHAPTER FOUR

The Roer Valley

12 November — 13 December 1944

The Allied Supreme Commander had directed that the enemy should be given no chance to reorganise in the west during the winter of 1944 and that therefore the offensive should be maintained unceasingly along the whole Allied front from Basle to Antwerp. Thus, the task of 12 US Army Group in November was to advance against Cologne with the First US Army, while the Ninth US Army protected its left flank. On the extreme right flank of 21 Army Group, 30 Corps was to capture Geilenkirchen and thereby facilitate the passage of the Ninth US Army to Linnich.

For this operation (known as operation Clipper) 30 Corps had the following formations under command: —

        Guards Armd Div
        43 Div
        84 US Div (less 335 RCT)
        113 US Cavalry Group
        8 Armd Bde
        79 Armd Div (four squadrons)
        5 AGRA.

On 12 November, 30 Corps took over command of its sector of the front which extended from exclusive Geilenkirchen to inclusive Maeseyck and by 15 November, 43 Div and Guards Armd Div had taken over their own sectors from American formations.

The Corps Commander's plan for operation Clipper was to encircle Geilenkirchen by attacks from the northwest and southeast, delivered by 43 Div and 84 US Div respectively. His plan was divided into the following four phases: — See Map 23.

Phase I

Capture of Prummern by 84 US Div, followed by despatch of patrols to Wurm valley.

Phase II

Capture of area Bauchem — Niederheide — Tripsrath by 43 Div, followed by despatch of patrols to Wurm valley to contact 84 US Div.

Phase III

Capture of Geilenkirchen by 84 US Div.

Phase IV

Capture of Straeten and Waldenrath by 43 Div, followed by exploitation to high ground south of Heinsburg.

D day for the 30 Corps attack was dependent on the progress made by Ninth US Army, and was to be fixed later. It was planned that Phase I of the operation should start at 0730 hrs on D day and that the subsequent phases should be so timed that the Corps artillery could support each phase in turn. Medium bombers and RP Typhoons would also be available to support the attack.

The enemy dispositions at this time, together with those positions of the Siegfried Line which lay opposite the Corps front, are shown on Map 23. Originally the enemy line was held by 183 Inf Div, but during the course of the battle both 15 Pz Gr and 10 SS Pz Div were committed against the Corps.

The joint Allied offensive opened on 15 November when 12 British Corps attacked west of the Maas and on the following day the American Armies commenced their drive to Cologne.

Phase I of operation Clipper began in the dark early morning of 18 November. Supported by a heavy artillery programme and considerable air support, 334 RCT of 84 US Div started at 0730 hrs to

MAP 22

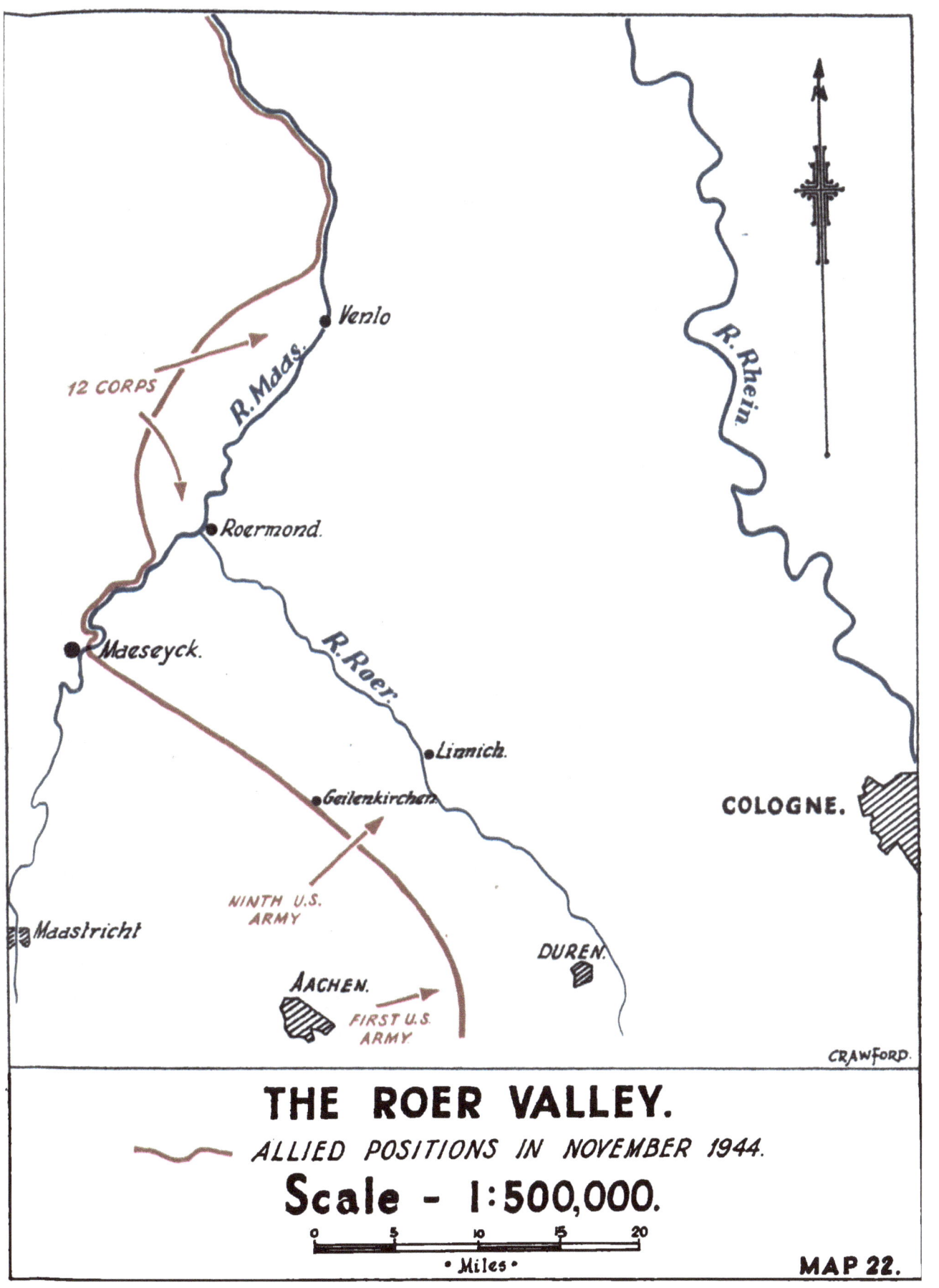

MAP 23

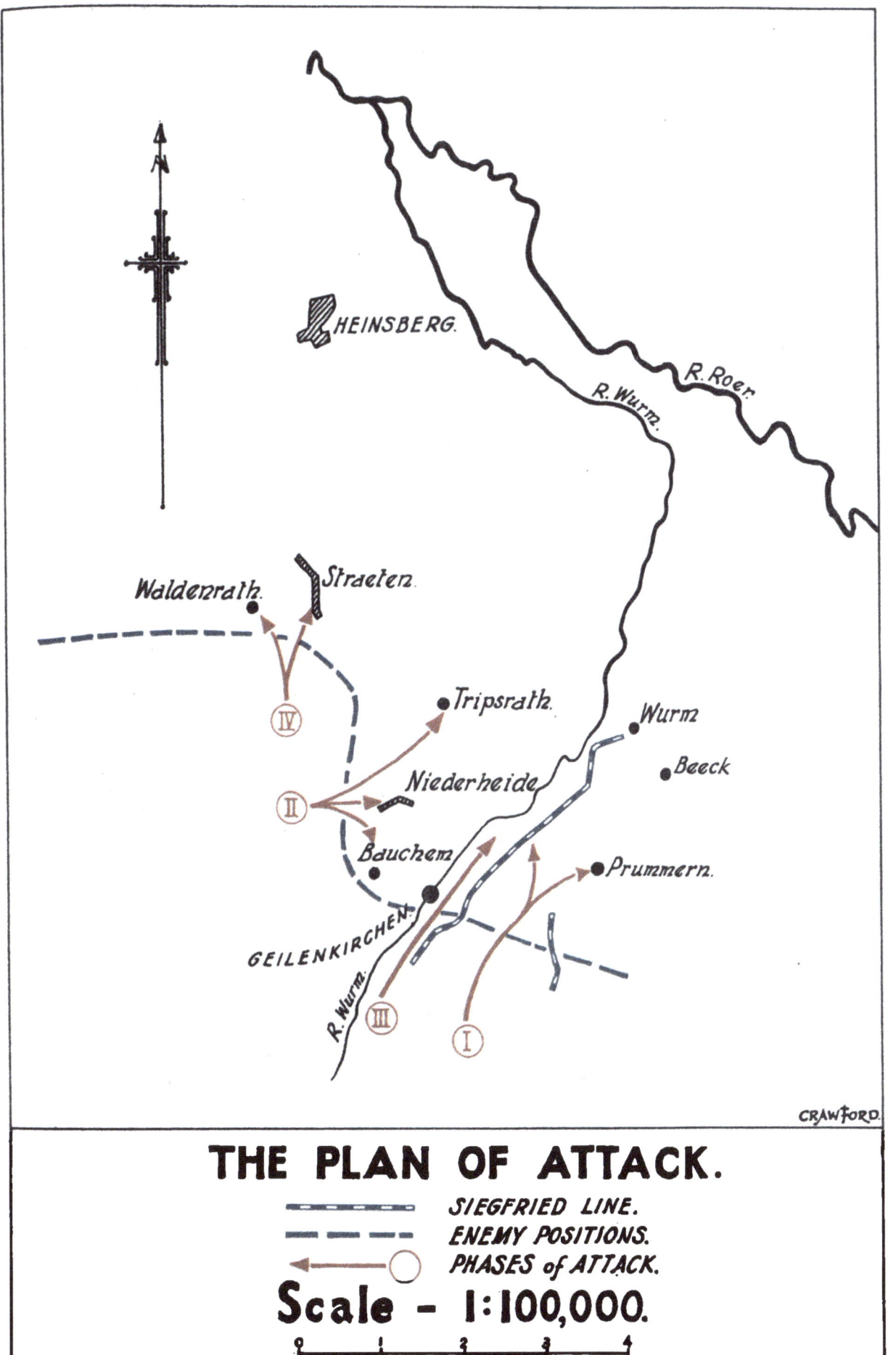

THE PLAN OF ATTACK.

–––––– SIEGFRIED LINE.
– – – ENEMY POSITIONS.
⟵ ◯ PHASES of ATTACK.

Scale - 1:100,000.

· Miles ·

MAP 23.

force two gaps through the enemy minefields southeast of Geilenkirchen. This combat team was closely supported by SRY of 8 Armd Brigade and by elements of 79 Armd Div. The assault made a good start but at first only one crossing could be made across the defiles which lay in the path of our advance.

During the morning as the attack progressed, resistance strengthened, especially from some of the concrete pillboxes which were encountered. The enemy manning these pillboxes elected to remain within them until the tanks had passed and then rushed out to nearby foxholes to engage the approaching infantry. But our tanks soon observed this ruse and turning on their tracks engaged the exposed enemy at close quarters and did great slaughter; many tanks had exhausted their stock of Besa ammution before noon.

The attack proceeded almost exactly as planned and by 1600 hrs Prummern was captured and American patrols moved forward to the Wurm valley.

Meanwhile, shortly after midday, Phase II of the operation had been commenced by 43 Div. Supported by 4/7 DG, 214 Inf Brigade launched a series of attacks on the west flank. All these were successful and Bauchem, Bruggerhof, Hochheid, Niederheide and Tripsrath were captured.

At the end of the day, the two Divisions had gained all the Corps objectives and had taken 800 prisoners. Patrols had made contact in the Wurm valley and Geilenkirchen was virtually isolated.

The attack was resumed early on 19 November by 333 RCT of 84 US Div. Supported by one squadron of SRY and elements of 79 Armd Div., it advanced up the Wurm valley from Frelenburg towards Geilenkirchen. Although there was little opposition, progress was not fast owing to the multitude of mines and booby traps. But gradually the valley was cleared and Geilenkirchen was entered. Those enemy who attempted to escape up the valley were given a warm reception by the troops of 214 Inf Brigade and 334 RCT, who were in contact northeast of the town. Many were killed and 200 were taken prisoner. 333 RCT continued their advance through Geilenkirchen until they made contact with 43 Div in the Bruggerhof area.

On the right flank, 334 RCT had a hard day's fighting north of Prummern. It successfully repelled counter attacks by at least one battalion of 15 Pz Gr Div, supported by some Tiger tanks and then, overcoming strong opposition, it pushed forward a battalion to the high ground northeast of Prummern. During the day this combat team knocked out six tanks. On their left flank, 43 Div began its attack against Hoven and started to clear the woods between Hatterath and Tripsrath.

By now, the continual rain had turned all the battle area into a quagmire and movement by tanks across country had become virtually impossible. In fact, the appalling going now exerted a marked effect on the battle, for by limiting the use of tanks, it prevented our early gains being further exploited.

The 20 November was chiefly spent in mopping up and consolidating. 84 US Div successfully beat off several counter attacks which were launched from the northeast and 43 Div completed the clearance of the woods north of Hatterath and repulsed a counter attack against Tripsrath.

During the day 250 prisoners were taken, bringing the total captured during the operation to over 1,300.

On 21 November, 84 US Div put in an attack to capture Wurm and Beeck. Very heavy opposition was encountered from 15 Pz Gr Div and in spite of most bitter fighting little progress could be made except on the extreme right, where one American battalion managed to reach the high ground east of Beeck.

The following day, 84 US Div (with 405 RCT now under command) resumed its attacks on Wurm and Beeck. Better progress was made this day and a battalion reached the high ground northeast of Beeck, while another reached the southern outskirts of the village. On the left, 333 RCT pushed about one mile up the Wurm valley from Suggerath. West of the valley, 43 Div was committed in heavy fighting, as a result of which 5 DCLI succeeded in capturing Hoven.

The 23 November was a day of counter attacks. A very powerful attack was put in by 10 SS Pz Div against Hoven and the forward company of 5 DCLI was cut off. After a bitter engagement, Hoven had to be abandoned. On the right flank, two other battalions of 10 SS Pz Div attacked and recaptured the American positions northeast of Beeck. In the centre, an attempt by the enemy to penetrate down the

MAP 24

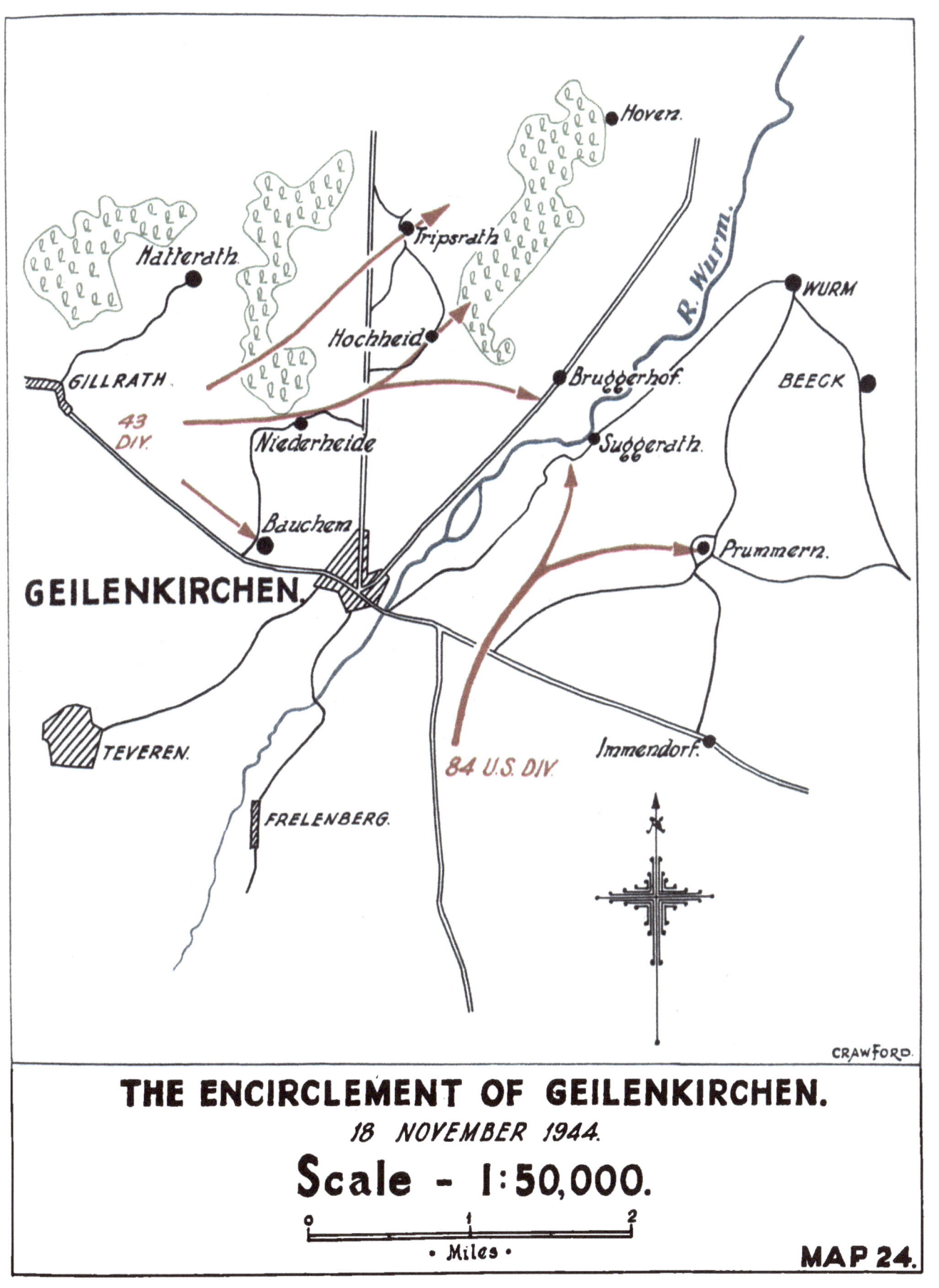

THE ENCIRCLEMENT OF GEILENKIRCHEN.
18 NOVEMBER 1944.
Scale - 1:50,000.

MAP 24.

MAP 25

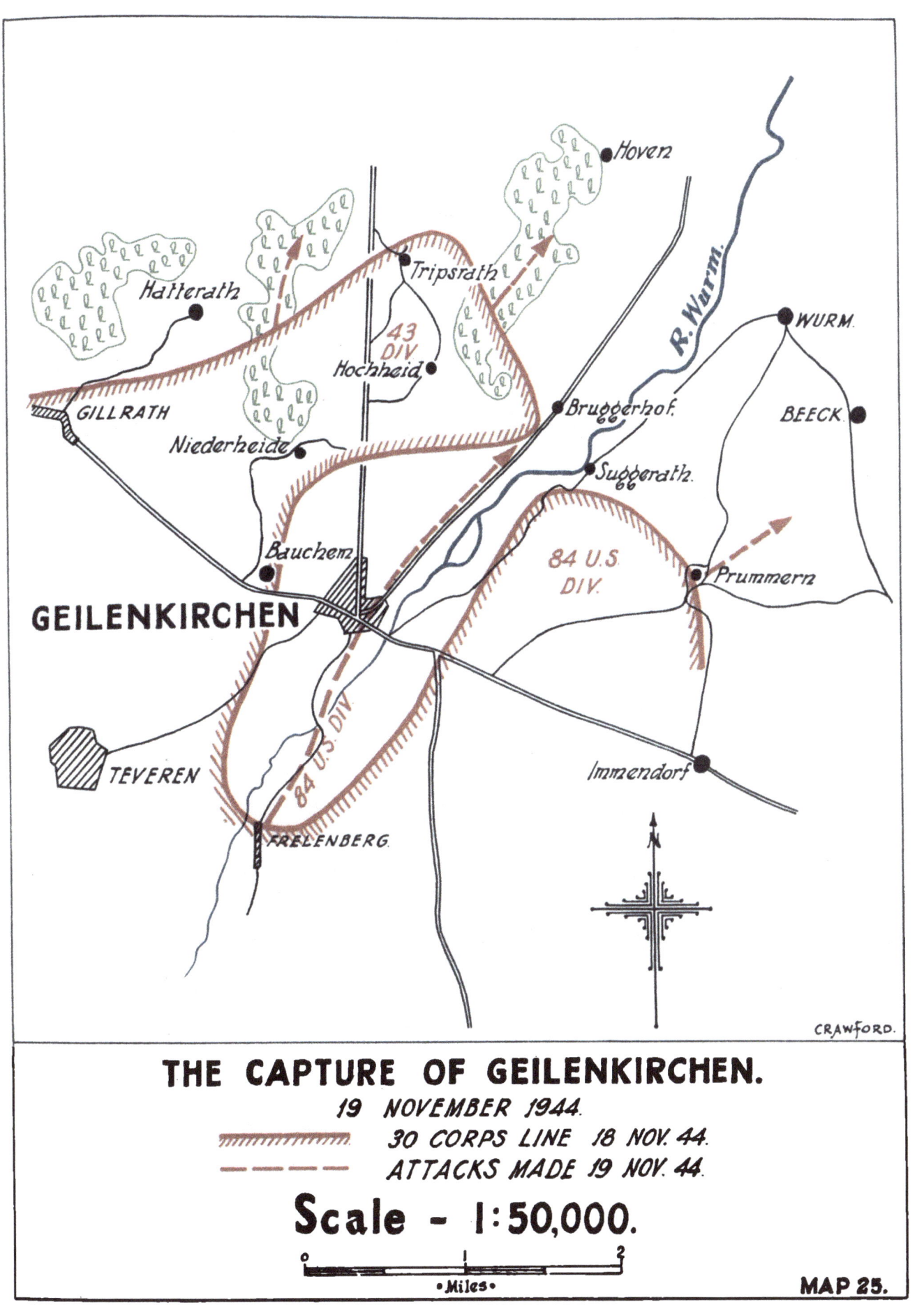

THE CAPTURE OF GEILENKIRCHEN.
19 NOVEMBER 1944.
30 CORPS LINE 18 NOV. 44.
ATTACKS MADE 19 NOV. 44.

Scale - 1:50,000.

MAP 25.

Wurm valley towards Suggerath was successfully sealed off. However, none of these attacks loosened the Corps' hold on Geilenkirchen, the original objective of the operation, and at 1800 hrs, 23 November, with the battle turning to the defensive, 84 US Div reverted to command XIII US Corps.

For the remainder of the month, activity on the 30 Corps front was mainly confined to patrols. A particularly successful raid was carried out on 26 November by 43 Div. A party of enemy had obstinately retained a hold on some school buildings at the northern end of Tripsrath and their liquidation was entrusted to 5 Wilts. A short sharp artillery bombardment was put down on the school and immediately it lifted the assault party rushed in — before the enemy had a chance to come out of his shelters. 50 prisoners were taken; 5 Wilts suffered only 4 wounded.

On 30 November, Field Marshal Sir Bernard Montgomery visited the Corps and saw his troops in action on the German soil, which they had so recently captured. During the day, he decorated men of 43 Div and 8 Armd Brigade and visited many units in the forward areas.

At this time, planning was started for an operation which was designed to clear the enemy from all the ground south of the Roer. But although all plans, including the artillery programmes, were prepared, this was an operation which 30 Corps was never to conduct. For on 13 December, in the greatest secrecy, Corps HQ moved back to Holland to plan again an assault on the Reichswald Forest.

CHAPTER FIVE

The Battle of the Ardennes

The German Offensive (Map 26)

By moving to Boxtel, Holland, on 13 December 1944, Main Corps HQ came out of contact with the enemy for the first time since D Day, more than six months earlier. Planning was immediately set in hand for operation Veritable, which was designed to destroy the enemy between the Rhine and the Maas. This operation was planned to commence early in January, 1945; in fact it did not begin until February. (A full account of the operation is given in a later chapter.)

In the planning rooms at Boxtel, news was received on 16 December that German Army Group B had that morning launched an attack against the First US Army between Duren and Trier. It soon became clear that the scope of this attack and the surprise it achieved far surpassed anything launched by the Wehrmacht in the West since 1940. The attacks on the first day were to some extent feints for bigger things to come. In the south, the enemy crossed the river Our and succeeded in isolating Echternach. Further north, he made two thrusts across the frontiers of Belgium and Luxembourg.

The big attack began on 17 December. Parachutists were dropped over large areas from north of Aachen to north of Malmedy; their role was mainly diversionary and most of them were quickly mopped up. Meanwhile, the main forces pushed westwards; 1 SS Pz Corps by-passed Malmedy and further south 11 Pz and 116 Pz Divs reached St Vith and encircled the town, and 2 Pz Div captured Clervaux.

On 18 December, except at Monschau which was recaptured by the Americans, the momentum of the enemy offensive showed no signs of slackening. 1 SS Pz Corps reached Stavelot; 116 Pz Div reached Vielsalm and Pz Lehr Div captured Wiltz. By now the enemy had committed nineteen divisions and although his object was not yet revealed it appeared that he might be making a bold bid to recapture Brussels and Antwerp.

By 19 December, the bulk of the enemy forces operating in the offensive had been identified. It was established that the attack by Army Group B had been launched with right 6 SS Army and left 5 Pz Army. By this date they had broken into the American front as far as Stavelot and Bastogne, though both these places were still held by US troops. Meanwhile at "the shoulders" of the breakthrough the Americans stubbornly held out near Monschau and Echternach and several pockets of isolated Americans were known to be still fighting in the St Vith area.

It was appreciated at this time that the enemy would now attempt to "bounce" the Meuse crossings on a wide front and captured maps revealed his thrust lines crossing the river between Namur and Liège.

At about 1800 hrs, 19 December, 30 Corps received orders to move south with the Guards Armd Div, 43 and 53 Divs under command. Five hours later Main Corps HQ, abandoning its planning of operation Veritable, left Boxtel to take its part in the Battle of the Ardennes.

The Defence of Brussels (Map 27)

On 20 December, 30 Corps was positioned by Field Marshal Sir Bernard Montgomery (now commanding all forces north of the breakthrough) to deal with any enemy crossings of the Meuse and to strike offensively against any approach by the enemy towards Brussels. The tasks of its formations may be summarised as follows: —

Guards Armd Div to position themselves in the area Tirlemont, Diest, St Trond, to place a strong recce screen along the Meuse from Huy to Charleroi, and to be prepared to counter attack any enemy force crossing the Meuse.

43 Div to position themselves in the area Tongres, Hasselt, Bilsen, to place a strong recce screen along the Meuse from Huy to Vise, and to be prepared to counter attack any enemy force crossing the Meuse.

MAP 26

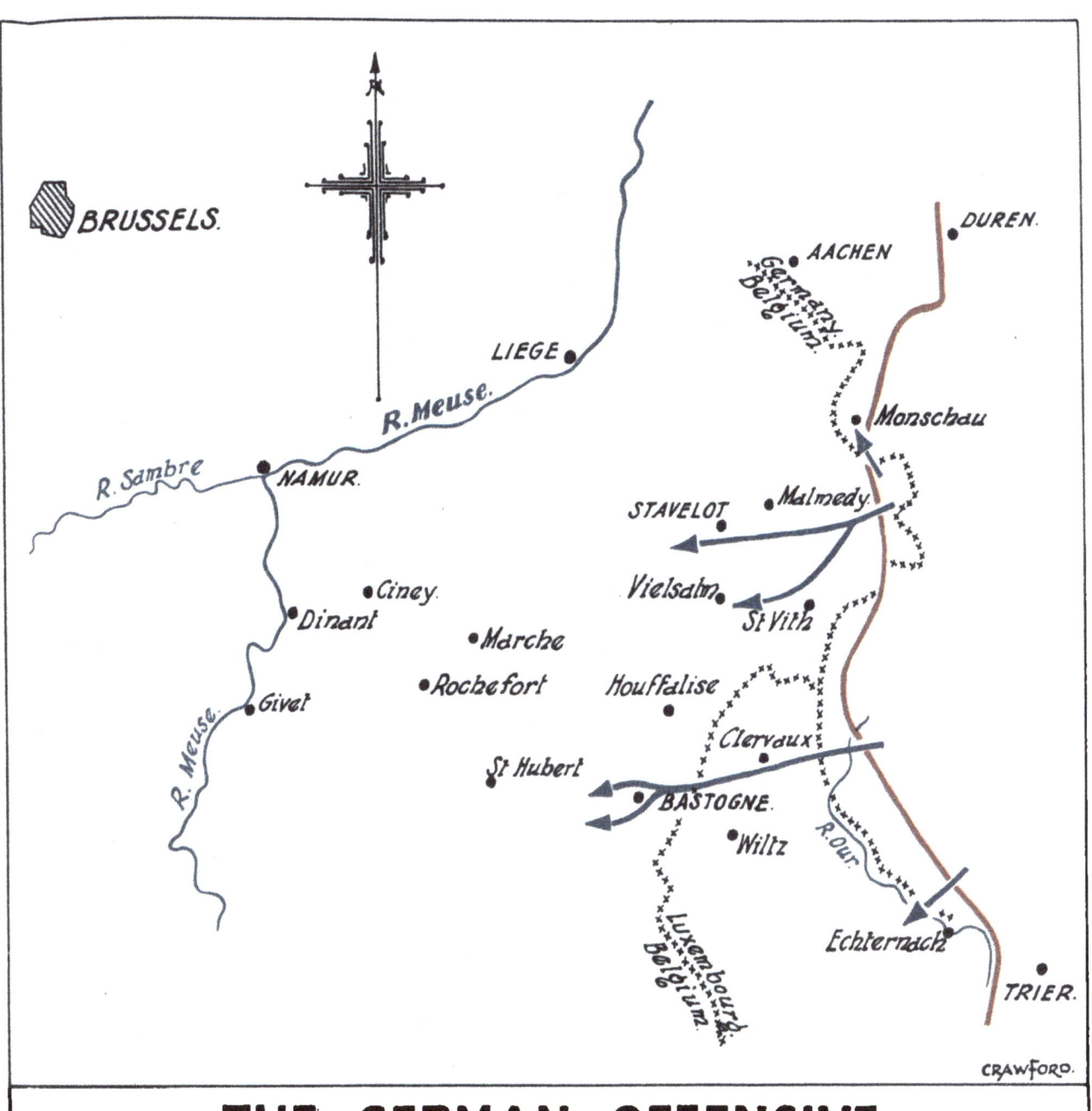

<u>53 Div</u> to establish a firm base for the Corps in the Louvain area holding the line of river Dyle from Ottignies to Louvain.

Later that day 51 Div also came under command and was held in Corps reserve in the area of Louvain and Aerschot. 30 Corps HQ was established at Hasselt.

On 21 December, 29 Armd Brigade was placed under command 53 Div and was directed to prevent the enemy crossing the Meuse or capturing any bridges between Givet and Namur. The Brigade moved into position on this day but made no contact with the enemy. The Americans were engaged in heavy fighting between Monschau and Stavelot and around Bastogne. Their resistance at Monschau had successfully frustrated the enemy intention of reaching Liège and the denial of Bastogne had hindered the enemy advance along the southern axis of their offensive. The main result of this magnificent resistance by the Americans was virtually to have destroyed all hopes of the enemy "to bounce" the Meuse crossings.

<u>The Defence of the Meuse</u>

The role of 30 Corps, now that the threat to Brussels had been reduced, was to prevent the enemy crossing the Meuse between Givet and Vise (excluding the American sector at Liège). Patrols of 2 HCR were accordingly despatched south and east of the river on 22 December but they made no contact with the enemy. The recce screens along the river were strengthened and every bridge was prepared for demolition and was strongly garrisoned. 29 Armd Brigade Group reverted to Corps command.

Meanwhile, the enemy offensive lost nothing in its ferocity, even though its territorial gains were not spectacular. Stavelot was captured by the enemy and then lost to him by an American counter attack. Bastogne, still isolated, had been by-passed and the enemy was moving southwards from the town. By dint of committing his reserve corps, 2 Pz Corps, the enemy had succeeded in capturing St Vith and this had opened the possibility of continuing his main thrust in a westerly direction from this area.

The deepest penetration towards the Meuse was made on 21 December by 2 Pz Div which attempted to encircle Marche and succeeded in capturing Ciney. It was in this area that patrols of 29 Armd Bde made their first contact with the enemy; only patrols were encountered and no decisive action was fought. Further south, Pz Lehr Div attacked St Hubert but failed to capture the town. To the north 2 US Armd Div was engaged in a series of tank battles round Celles, while 84 US Div halted 116 Pz Div outside Marche. The enemy intentions appeared to remain unchanged: 6 SS Army intending to reach the Meuse at Liège and 5 Pz Army pushing out to Namur.

On 24 December, 5 Pz Army made further progress in its advance to the Meuse and its patrols almost reached the river at Dinant. Thus in nine days since the start of his offensive the enemy had broken through to a depth of 50 miles. 29 Armd Brigade was engaged in a fierce skirmish this day between Conneux and Celles about six miles east of Dinant, where it encountered a company of enemy infantry and some dozen tanks. Five enemy tanks were destroyed in the engagement and the enemy group withdrew. Further south Pz Lehr Div captured St Hubert and was reported to be making for Givet. At this point the German command appears to have modified its plan of campaign, and it appeared as though he might now attempt to make his main thrust in the Namur area instead of as originally planned at Liège.

On Christmas Day, 71 Inf Brigade took over the Meuse bridges south of Namur thereby releasing 29 Armd Brigade to operate east of the river. During the day contact was re-established with the enemy, this time in the area of Foy Notre Dame, and in a spirited engagement 29 Armd Brigade knocked out half a dozen enemy vehicles and captured 100 prisoners from 2 Pz Div. Elsewhere the main battle raged round Bastogne, against which the enemy had now deployed no less than four divisions against the 101 US Airborne Div, who still held out in the town undaunted by the odds against them.

The first brigade of 6 Airborne Division (which had arrived from England to come under command of the Corps) took over the Meuse crossings from 71 Inf Brigade on 26 December 1944. No contact was made with the enemy on the Corps front this day, as 2 Pz Div had deemed it prudent to withdraw slightly after its setback at Foy Notre Dame on Christmas Day. There was little change anywhere on the Ardennes front, except that 9 Pz Div captured Humain between Rochefort and Marche.

MAP 27

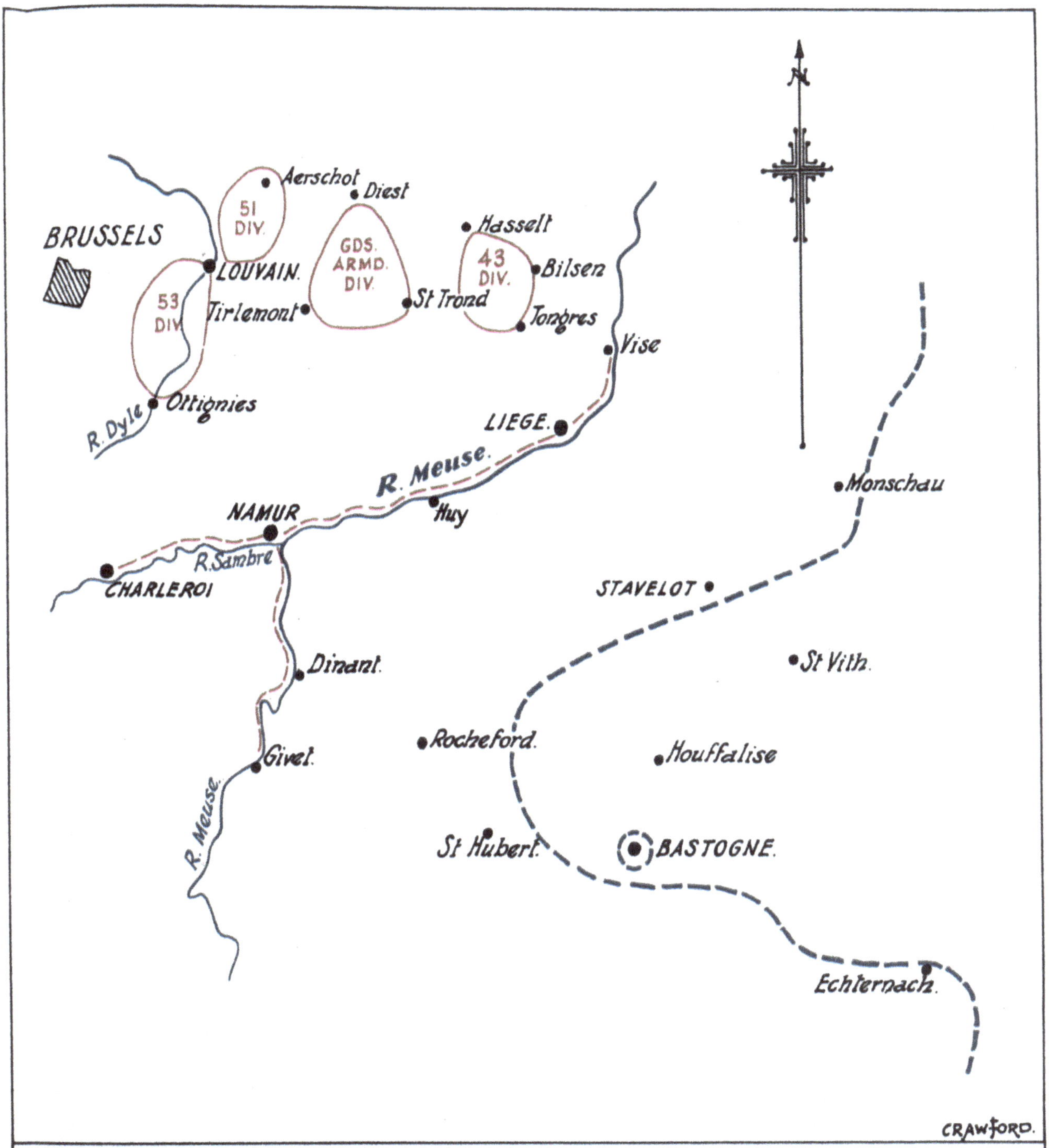

THE DEFENCE OF BRUSSELS.

◯   30 CORPS DISPOSITIONS
— — —   30 CORPS RECCE SCREEN
— —   APPROX. ENEMY LINE 21 DEC.

Scale – 1:1,000,000.

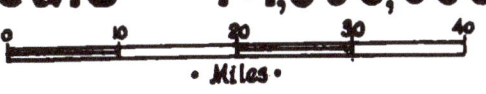

MAP 27.

MAP 28

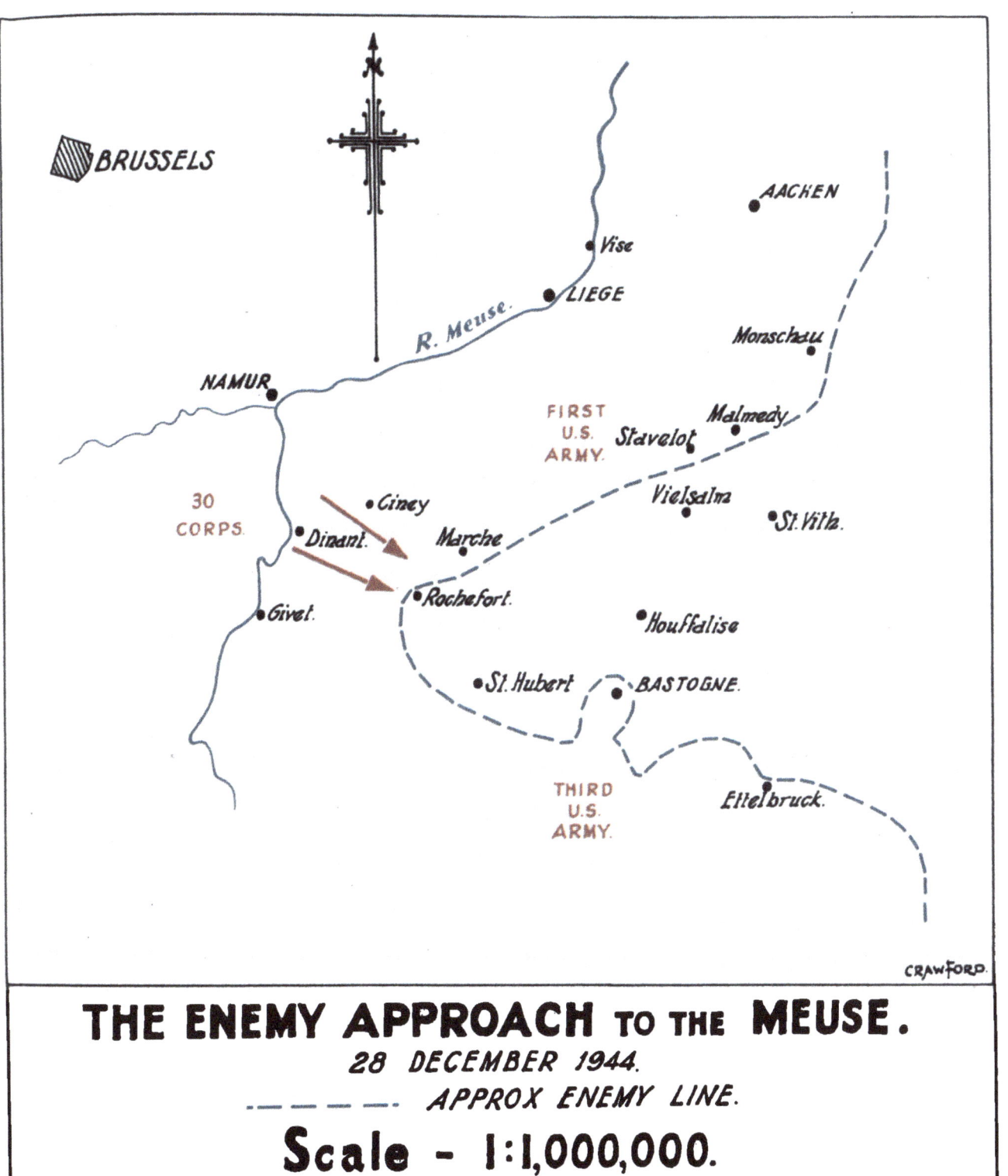

MAP 29

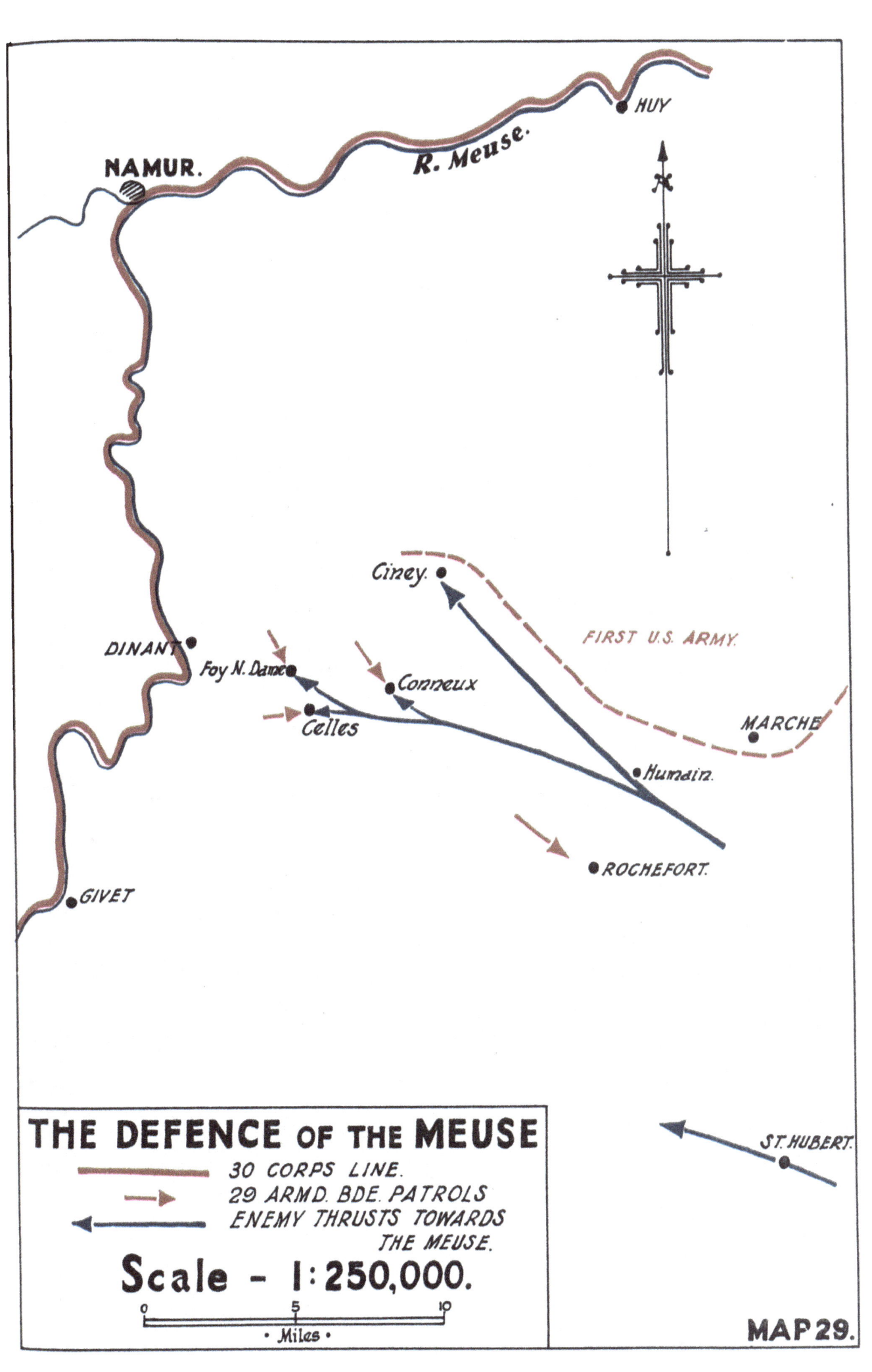

The 27 December saw the first real defeat inflicted on the enemy on the Corps front in this offensive. In conjunction with 2 US Armd Div, 29 Armd Brigade engaged a strong battle group of 2 Pz Div in the area of Celles. The joint British-American "bag" in this engagement was 1,500 prisoners captured and 110 vehicles and 24 AFVs brewed up. In consequence 2 Pz Div withdrew towards Rochefort and the immediate threat to the Meuse was lifted.

On the 27 December, 6 Airborne Div completed its takeover of the Meuse crossings from 53 Div, and 43 Div moved east to Maastricht, passing to command of 12 Corps.

From 28 December onwards the enemy showed little signs of aggression on the Corps front. The effect of the stubborn defence of the main keypoints by the Americans, together with heavy bombing of the German main axis, had definitely stopped the momentum of the offensive. From this point onwards the enemy began to withdraw from the western tip of the salient and our patrols entered Rochefort on 30 December. The threat to the Meuse was now unquestionably over.

The German withdrawal (Maps 30, 31 and 32)

On 1 January 1945, the Allies turned to the offensive. It was planned that a joint attack should be made by First and Third US Armies, from the north and south of "the bulge", both directed upon Houffalise. In order to enable the First US Army to get on a narrow front, Field Marshal Sir Bernard Montgomery ordered 30 Corps to take over the sector Hotton—Rochefort. 53 (W) Div accordingly took over this part of the front and the 84 and 2 Armd US Divs (previously holding this sector) sidestepped eastwards. 30 Corps was directed to attack in unison with First US Army and to keep abreast with 84 US Div on its left.

Meanwhile, south of the river Lesse, 6 Airborne Div (with 29 Armd Brigade under command) had been ordered to operate offensively on the general axis Givet—St Hubert. This thrust encountered extremely heavy resistance from Pz Lehr Div and in spite of heavy fighting it proved impossible to capture Bure.

The powerful American attacks commenced in a driving blizzard at 0830 hrs on 3 January. Small gains were made all along the First US Army front but the weather prevented any spectacular successes.

It snowed continuously and all the roads were icebound; the weather had now become our worst enemy.

It was evident, however, that the Panzer Corps opposing 30 Corps would not long be able to hold its positions, with the Americans threatening both its flanks; there were in fact already signs of its withdrawing back to the river Ourthe.

Early on 4 January, 53 Div launched its attack between the river Ourthe and the main road running southeast from Marche. Opposition on the whole was slight, the chief obstacles to our advance being mines and booby traps in the snow. During the afternoon two counter attacks were repulsed and by evening, gains averaging about two miles had been made. 97 prisoners, all from 116 Pz Div, were captured.

On the right sector of the Corps, 6 Airborne Div was still heavily committed in Bure, which was finally reported clear late in the evening; Wavreille still held out.

Extremely heavy fighting raged right along the Corps front throughout 5 January. 53 Div was unable to make any progress up the Ourthe valley and on its right flank heavy enemy counter attacks recaptured almost all the ground gained earlier in the day. Two determined attempts were made by the enemy to recapture Bure from 6 Airborne Div. On the American sector, slight advances were reported in the north, but the American attacks around Bastogne had been halted.

Little progress was made on 30 Corps front on 6 January, but on the First US Army sector advances were made in the area Vielsaem and Stavelot. An important tactical success was gained on 7 January, when 53 Div captured Grimbiemont and the high ground to the northeast, thereby denying to the enemy the use of the La Roche—Marche road.

On 8 January, on which date 51 Div relieved 53 Div in the Marche—Hotton sector, there were definite signs that the enemy was withdrawing on the Corps front, and the villages of Jemelle, Marloie and Waharday were all found empty during the day. To the east, the Americans continued their advance towards Houffalise. For the next seventy-two hours there was virtually no contact on the Corps front, and the forward moves of 6 Airborne and 51 Divs were hampered only by the snow and ice, mines and bad going. As a result, the west bank of the river Ourthe was cleared almost down to La Roche and many

MAP 30

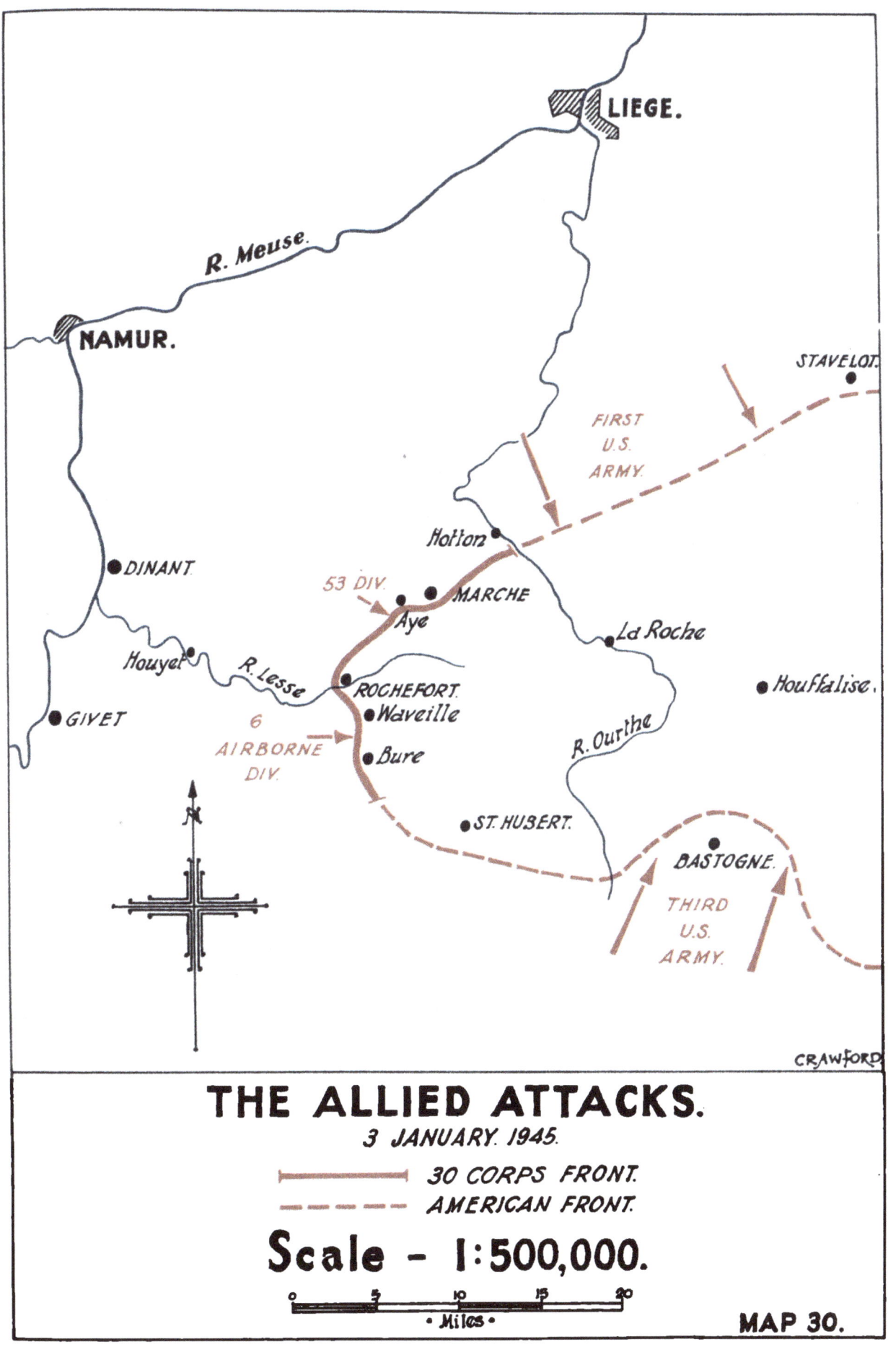

THE ALLIED ATTACKS.
3 JANUARY. 1945.

— 30 CORPS FRONT.
--- AMERICAN FRONT.

Scale — 1:500,000.

MAP 30.

MAP 31

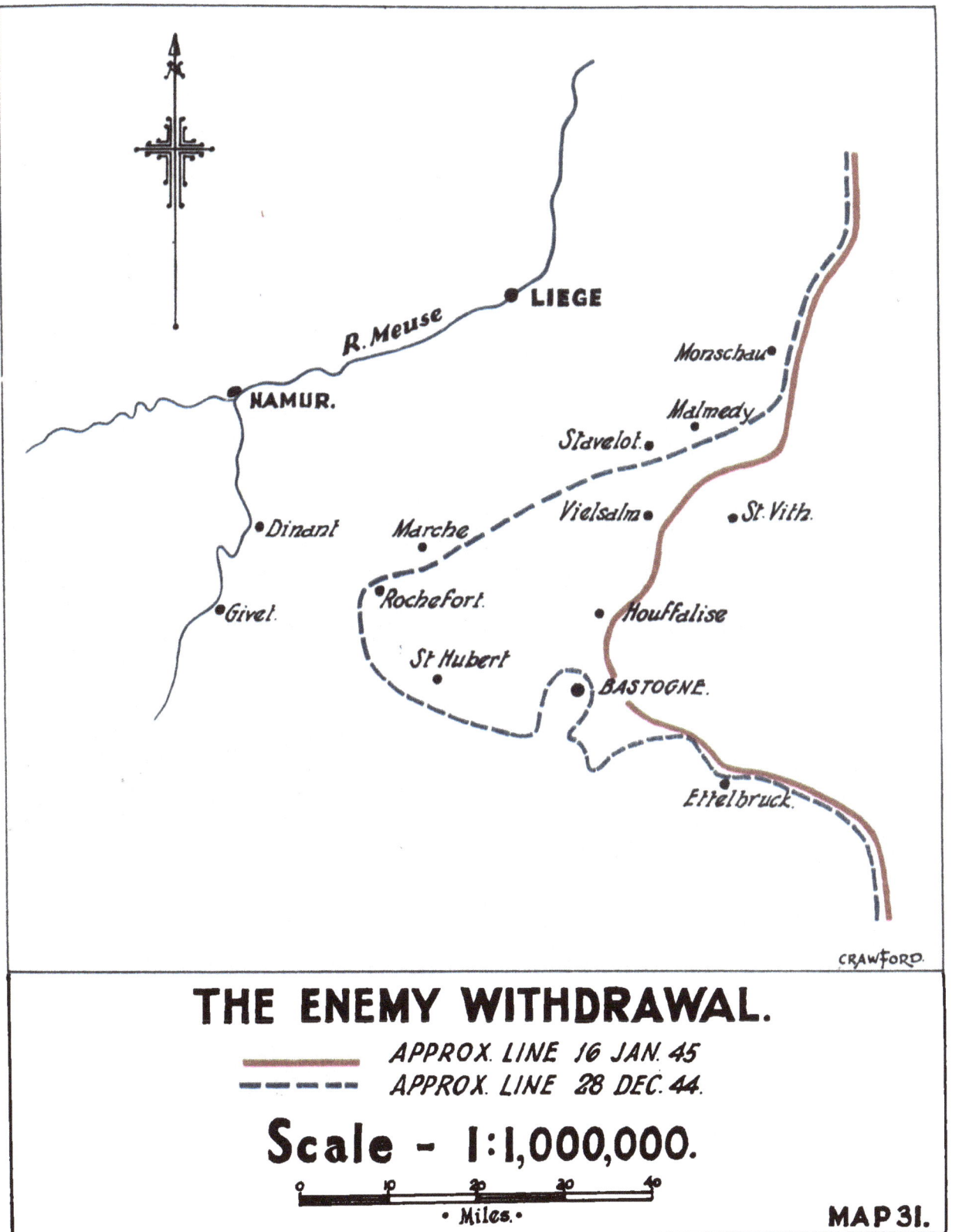

THE ENEMY WITHDRAWAL.

APPROX. LINE 16 JAN. 45
APPROX. LINE 28 DEC. 44.

Scale - 1:1,000,000.

MAP 31.

villages were captured. The enemy quickened the pace of his withdrawal on 11 January and only at La Roche was any contact made with the enemy. Our leading troops reached Hives during the day and patrols of 6 Airborne Div advanced within a few hundred yards of the Champlon crossroads.

On 12 January a marked change was noted in the enemy's tactics opposite the Corps front. After several days during which contact had been on the verge of being lost completely, it became evident that on the left sector the enemy's rearguards had turned to fight. 154 Inf Brigade of 51 Div was held up south of Hives by a strong force of infantry and tanks, and an enemy post east of Hives denied to us the use of the La Roche—Bastogne road. To the south, however, the enemy's withdrawal continued and the woods south of Champlon were found to be clear. The First US Army continued its steady advance and made further headway towards Houffalise. The Third US Army gained further successes round Bastogne, capturing 1200 prisoners in the day's operations.

2 Pz Div fought stubbornly on 13 January against 51 Div, and denied us the village of Nisramont until late in the day. Further west 51 Div captured Orthe and sent patrols to Cens. During the day some 65 prisoners were taken. The most important success on the American front was the cutting of the Houffalise—St Vith road, which blocked one of the enemy's main escape routes.

By 14 January, the Corps had cleared all the enemy from the area bounded on the northeast by the river Ourthe and on the south by its tributary the Ourthe Occidentale. Contact was made all along the latter with troops of the Third US Army. Meanwhile the converging attacks of the First and Third US Armies came together and on 16 January firm contact was made along the Ourthe to the west of Houffalise. Thus ended 30 Corps' share in the battle of the Ardennes.

MAP 32

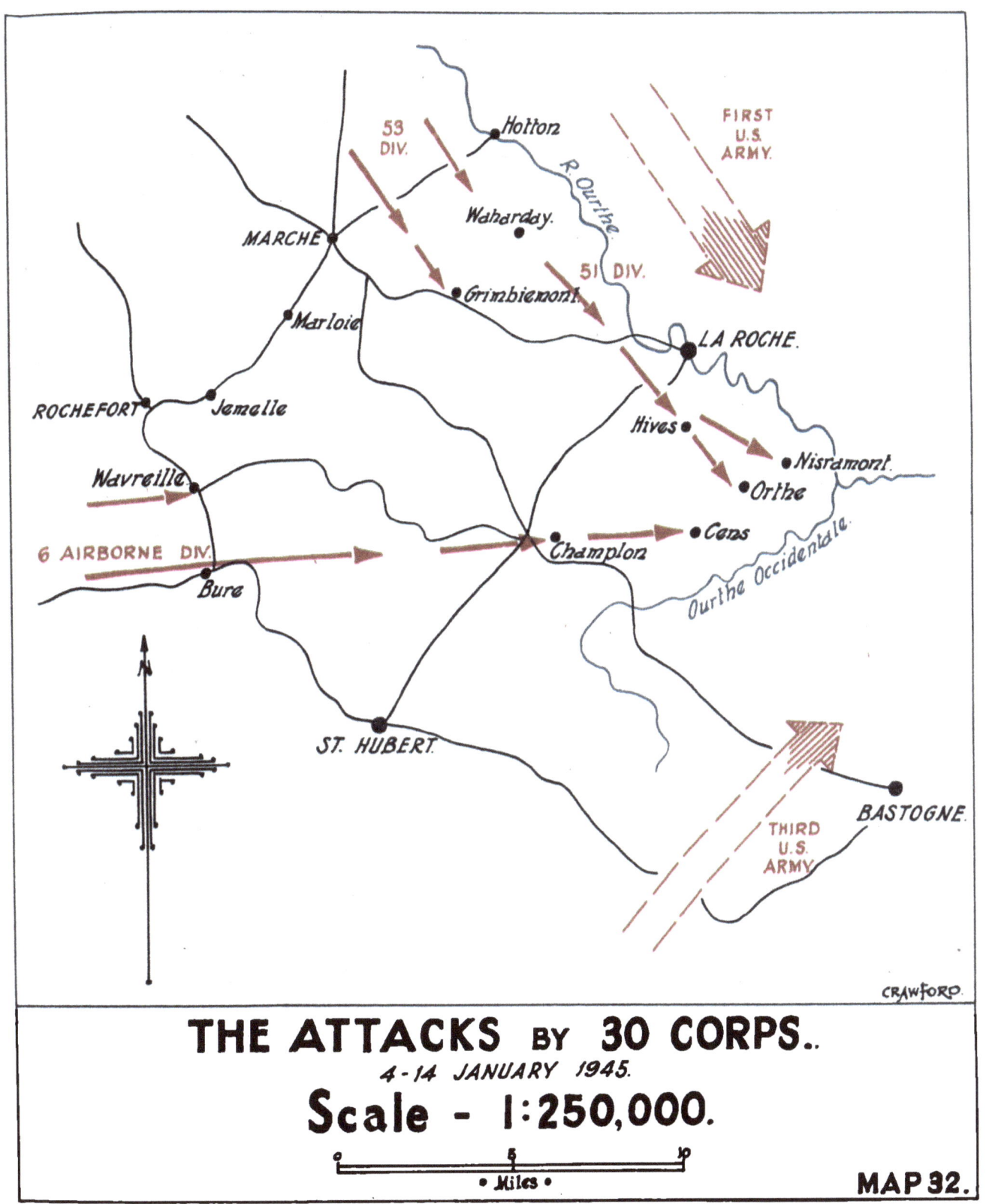

THE ATTACKS BY 30 CORPS.
4-14 JANUARY 1945.
Scale - 1:250,000.

MAP 32.

CHAPTER SIX

The Reichswald Battle

Operation veritable

The finish of the British fighting in the Ardennes released HQ 30 Corps to resume once again the planning of Operation Veritable, the object of which was to destroy the enemy between the R. Maas and the R. Rhine. When this task was completed, 21 Army Group would be poised ready to cross the Rhine and to break into the heart of Germany.

For the opening of the attack, 30 Corps* (which was under command of First Canadian Army for this operation) would comprise the biggest concentration of troops yet assembled by 21 Army Group under one Corps, namely:—

One Armoured Division
Six Infantry Divisions
Three Armoured Brigades
Eleven regiments of 79 Armoured Div,
Five AGsRA

30 Corps strength was just over 200,000 all ranks.

The attack was to be staged from the Canadian positions between the Rhine and the Maas to the east of Nijmegen (Map 33).

At the outset, 9 US Army (also under command 21 Army Group) was to hold the R. Roer from Julich to Roermond but at a later date it would develop an offensive across the Roer, to link up with the

---

* 30 Corps Order of Battle is shown at Appendix "C"

30 Corps operation. The British Second Army was to hold the R. Maas from Cuyk to Roermond.

Though the enemy offensive in the Ardennes had been stemmed and then repulsed, there was no doubt that the Germans hoped to have staved off all threats of a major allied assault in the west. It was to mount just such an offensive and to regain the initiative in the west, that operation Veritable was staged. The Corps Commander appreciated that initially the operation would be successful and he therefore planned to exploit its success to the uttermost. If however exploitation proved impossible, he told his commanders that he was prepared to fight night and day, unceasingly, until the German Army in the North had been destroyed. The nature of the coming battle was forecast by Field Marshal Sir Bernard Montgomery in a personal message to his troops before the attack, from which the following extract is quoted: —

> "In 21 Army Group we stand ready for the last round... The rules of the last round will be that we continue fighting till the final count: there is no time limit. We know our enemy well; we must expect him to fight hard to stave off defeat, possibly in the vain hope that we may crack before he does. But we shall not crack; we shall see this thing through to the end. The last round may be long and difficult, and the fighting hard; but we now fight on German soil; we have got our opponent where we want him; and he is going to receive the knock-out blow; a somewhat unusual one, delivered from more than one direction."

Though the initial assault proved magnificently successful, the subsequent course of the battle was so influenced by weather conditions, especially by flooding, that rapid exploitation did not in fact prove possible. In the north the Germans blew the banks of the Rhine and succeeded in cutting one of the Corps main axis. Simultaneously in the south, the enemy blew the Roer dams and thus postponed the offensive by 9 US Army. This latter stratagem was perhaps the biggest single factor in slowing down the Corps advance. Realising that his southern flank was protected by the flooded Roer, the German Commander was able to switch all his reserves into the battle against 30 Corps. Consequently when the Americans advanced, on 23 February, there was only a thin screen of two enemy divisions to oppose them. Their advance was rapid and had the natural effect of loosening opposition against the Corps in the north. The cleaning up of the Wesel bridgehead quickly followed and, after four week's fighting, all objectives of the 21 Army Group operations were achieved.

The Plan

When planning of the operation commenced, three of the Corps' divisions were deployed in the area Namur—Liège after the Ardennes battle and one division and two armoured brigades were still fighting in the Geilenkirchen—Sittard area. It was clear therefore that the movement north and eventual concentration for this operation, in a limited time and with due regard to secrecy, would require most careful planning and control. Movement staffs were accordingly augmented and a large traffic control organisation, embracing some 1,600 men, was set up. Initially the indifferent roads were frostbound and later came the thaw with all its attendant troubles. Good roads deteriorated rapidly and others collapsed completely. Nevertheless, as if by a miracle, traffic control and movement staffs were able to report, at the appointed hour, that the assembly of some 200,000 men with their tanks and vehicles, guns and ammunition, had been successfully completed.

Veritable was the first operation, since the original landing on the Continent, where the British had to break into an unbreached series of prepared defences. Immediately in front of the foremost localities on the Nijmegen sector ran the strong outposts of the Siegfried Line. These were organised in two strongly held lines; the first from Kiekberg Woods to Wyler and the second from Gennep along the western edge of the Reichswald Forest to Kranenberg. The Siegfried Line itself lay some 3,500 yards east of our forward positions and consisted of many concrete fortifications, which had recently been reinforced by a labyrinth of field defences. The main belt of this line is shown on Map 34. In addition, a well designed anti-tank ditch had been dug from the Reichswald near Frasselt, through Kranenberg, northwards to the Alter Rhine. Further to the east was the "Hochwald lay-back"; an unbroken line of trenches and anti-tank ditches, which stretched from the Rhine opposite Rees, past the western side of the Hochwald and Balberger forests towards Geldern. Furthermore, pursuing his policy of "hedgehog defence", the enemy had split up the area into a series of selfcontained "boxes" and had transformed many of his towns and villages into strong points.

Opposite the Corps front were about eight enemy battalions, mostly from 84 Inf Div, with five battalions in reserve. The morale of these troops was rated as high and it was expected that they would be covered by at least one hundred guns. It was further estimated that the enemy would be able to reinforce this front within the first week of the attack by about three infantry and two panzer divisions.

The Corps Commander's intention was to attack with five infantry divisions up, namely:—

    From Right to Left: 51 (Highland) Division
                              53 (Welsh) Division
                              15 (Scottish) Division
                              2 Canadian Division
                              3 Canadian Division
    Reserve and Follow Up: Guards Armd Division
                              43 (Wessex) Division

In brief, the tasks delegated to divisions (Map 35) for the first day were:—

- 51 (H) Div to capture the southwest corner of the Reichswald and to prevent any enemy movement into the battle area from the south.
- 53 (W) Div to seize the high ground at the northwest corner of the Reichswald and then to move eastwards through the northern half of the forest.
- 15 (S) Div to capture Kranenberg and the high ground overlooking Cleve.
- 2 Cdn Div to capture Wyler.
- 3 Cdn Div to take Zifflich and Leuth and then drive eastwards to the Cleve—Alter Rhine Canal.

It was planned that exploitation after D Day should proceed as follows:—

- 15 (S) Div would clear Cleve and despatch mobile columns to capture Udem and Calcar and clear the Emmerich road to the west bank of the Rhine.

MAP 33

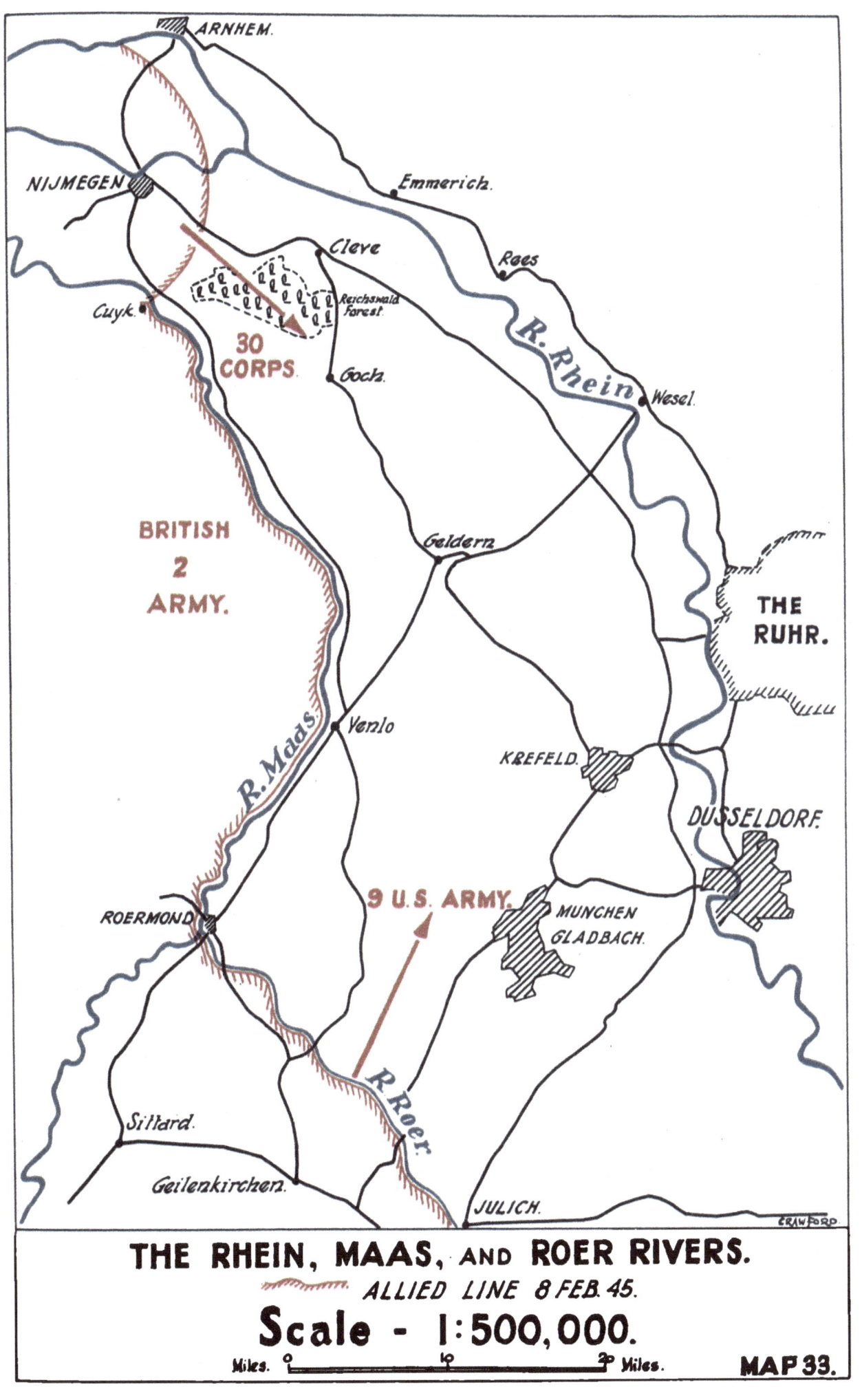

THE RHEIN, MAAS, AND ROER RIVERS.
ALLIED LINE 8 FEB. 45.
Scale - 1:500,000.

MAP 33.

MAP 34

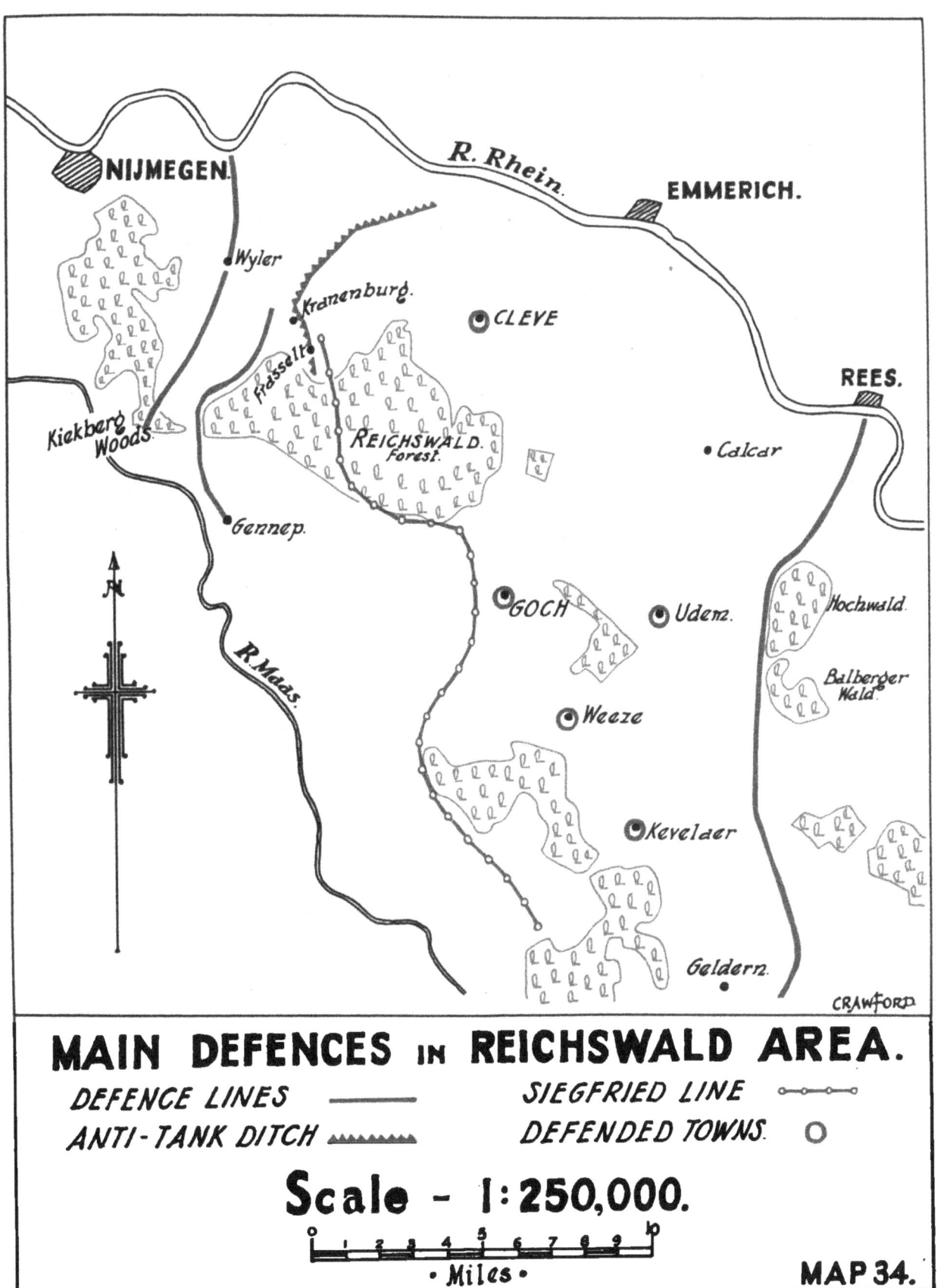

51 (H) Div was to attack Goch and 53 (W) Div was to clear the Reichswald.

43 Div would move forward on D + 1 and pass through 15 (S) Div and attack south from Goch.

Gds Armd Div was to follow 43 Div and then capture the high ground north of Sonsbeck, sending forward a strong column to seize the Wesel bridge.

The operation was to be supported by an overwhelming weight of artillery. With each successive operation, the Corps artillery had become more and more important as a battle winning factor and it was perhaps in Operation Veritable that it produced its most successful and devastating performance. Never before, in this War, had so many guns been deployed in support of a British Corps. No less than 1,000 field medium and heavy guns and 200 guns of smaller calibre were arrayed to take their part in the carefully prepared fire plan *. The programme for air support was also on a lavish scale. In addition to the whole resources of Second Tactical Air Force, the "heavies" of US 9 Bombardment Division and of Bomber Command were made available.

The Assault

The first week of February 1945 was spent in co-ordinating the final details of the Corps plan and in moving the assault troops and supporting guns into their battle positions. Then at 0500 hrs, 8 February, through the cold darkness of a winter's night, there crashed the opening salvo of a thousand guns. The clear sky was alight with the flickering glare of flashing guns and, overhead, tracer shells and rockets wove an intricate pattern of streaming light.

For five hours this bombardment continued to pour down upon the enemy lines and gun positions. The enemy defenders, with their signal lines cut and their road communications blocked, were gradually reduced to that "shell-happy" state which the Corps had ordained. Meanwhile the Scottish, Welsh and Canadian formations were moving up to their assault positions. At 1000 hrs as the opening line of the barrage came down, a solid bank of shell bursts cut across the damp valley and

---

* An outline of the fire plan is given at Appendix "D".

enveloped the enemy defences. At 1030 hrs, the barrage made its first slow movement eastwards and at this signal the assaulting infantry and tanks, crocodiles and flails moved forward. Thus began Operation Veritable. For more than twenty eight days, throughout each day and night, there was to be no respite in its fighting.

In spite of the many mines and the appalling state of the ground, the attack went well. The Corps artillery preparation had so numbed the enemy's will and ability to resist that little opposition was encountered and in particular no hostile shell or mortar impeded our advance. On the extreme right, the leading brigade of 51 (H) Div met stiffish resistance from the villages north of Keikberg woods but by the afternoon had captured their objectives. 53 (W) Div successfully secured the important feature at the northwest corner of the Reichswald and, by 1700 hrs, 15 (S) Div had captured Kranenburg. By nightfall, 2 Cdn Div had cleared the strongpoint of Wyler, and in the early evening, 3 Cdn Div in "Buffaloes" attacked across the northern floods and quickly took Zyfflich. By midnight, the Corps Commander knew that all the objectives for that day had been taken. Over 1,100 prisoners had been captured and five enemy battalions had been decimated. Our own casualties had been light and so far our principal difficulties had been bad going, mines and flooding.

On 9 February, formations pressed forward in accordance with the original Corps plan. At 0400 hrs, 15 (S) Div, with powerful artillery support made their assault on the Siegfried Line. As a preliminary to this operation, crossings had to be made over the anti-tank ditch, which lay astride the Kranenburg—Nutterden road. Five attempts were made during the night to breach this obstacle. Only one succeeded. But this had to suffice and through this solitary gap, two battalions were launched against the main enemy defences. They quickly captured Nutterden, taking 250 prisoners, and during the afternoon 44 Inf Brigade occupied the Materborn feature. The assault on the Siegfried Line had been successful. Meanwhile, 53 (W) Div, fighting in the forest without pause for 36 hrs, reached their final objectives on the high ground southwest of Materborn that evening. On the flanks, 51 (H) Div cut the Mook—Gennep road in two places and 3 Cdn Div, continuing their aquatic operations across the floods, captured Mehr, Niel and Millingen. During the day, 43 Div had been ordered forward and by midnight the leading troops of its 129 Inf Brigade had reached Nutterden.

This second day of the offensive had seen the initial successes magnificently exploited and a further 1,700 prisoners had been captured. The main enemy defences had been breached and fresh troops were positioned ready to push into the rear of the enemy positions. Four battalions of reinforcements had been committed by the enemy but these did not suffice even to make good his losses. However the effect of the appalling weather and ground conditions on the coming operations was already beginning to be seen. The solitary axis of 53 (W) Div gave way completely and had to be closed for repair. To the north, the Germans blew the banks of the Rhine and floods were beginning to lap against the Nijmegen—Cleve road, (the axis of 15 (S) Div) and if the water continued to rise this road too would become impassable.

The full effect of these abnormal conditions, coupled with the arrival of enemy paratroops, became apparent the following day, 10 February. 15 (S) Div, which had been ordered to clear the exits from Materborn for 43 Div, failed to capture the important road centre of Cleve, though by midnight 6 RSF had reached the centre of the town. On the right flank, 51 (H) Div met stiffening opposition and although it captured Ottersum and Aaldonk, it was clear that a major attack would have to be mounted to clear Gennep before the main axis, the Mook—Goch road, could be considered secure. 53 (W) Div managed to consolidate its positions in the Reichswald during the day and to make contact in the forest with patrols of 51 (H) Div. During the previous night, 9/10 February, 129 Inf Brigade which had been directed to push southwards to Goch as soon as the Materborn exits were clear, attempted to get through by the main road from Nutterden to Cleve. It unfortunately got involved in confused fighting in the darkness with paratroops on the outskirts of Cleve. Thus when daylight came, this force was committed holding a small leaguer, which was being attacked from all sides; a position from which it proved impossible quickly to disengage them.

By this time the enemy opposition was steadily hardening and, with rising waters of the Alter Rhine completely closing the northern axis, the Corps communication situation was gradually worsening. It was now realised that the original plans for exploiting the success of D Day must be changed. The Corps Commander, therefore, still keeping the original objectives in view, ordered 3 Cdn Div and 15 (S) Div to hold Cleve and Materborn respectively and directed 43 Div to secure the high ground east of Cleve Forest, prior to continuing the advance to Udem and Goch. 51 (H) Div, whose 153 Inf Brigade had captured Gennep by a brilliant assault crossing of the river Niers during the night 10/11 February was now ordered to secure the Gennep—Goch road as far eastwards as Kessel.

The Advance towards Goch (Map 37)

The next few days saw heavy fighting on both the eastern and southern outskirts of the Reichswald, especially against the two armoured formations which the enemy now committed against the Corps. The enemy intention at this time was to recapture Cleve with 116 Pz Div, while 15 Pz Gr Div protected the left flank of his Panzer Corps. In this attempt, he launched seven out of his eight available Panzer Grenadier battalions into the assault on a 5,000 yards front. But against these attacks, the full might of the Corps artillery was unleashed and this, together with the determined defence of the leading infantry, succeeded in breaking up all assaults. The Corps advance went slowly on. To the east of the forest, 43 Div which had repelled the brunt of the counter-attacks by 116 Pz Div, secured Hau and Bedburg. By nightfall on 13 February, 4 Wilts had been able to gain a footing on the high ground to the east of Cleve Forest. A strong counter-attack against this newly won position was staged the following morning but 4 Wilts held their ground. On the south, 51 (H) Div made good progress and, capturing the important cross roads at Hekkens from 20 Para Regiment, pushel some 3,000 yards further to the east. In the centre, 53 (W) Div received the full force of the 15 Pz Gr Div's attacks on 12 February but yielded no ground. Meanwhile 15 (S) Div, attempting to push a brigade group out to Calcar, encountered very fierce opposition and could only succeed in reaching Hasselt.

But important as these small advances were they did nothing to diminish the ferocity of the fighting and there now followed the most bitter period of the whole operation. The German Army had now plainly elected to fight west of the Rhine and it was here that he had

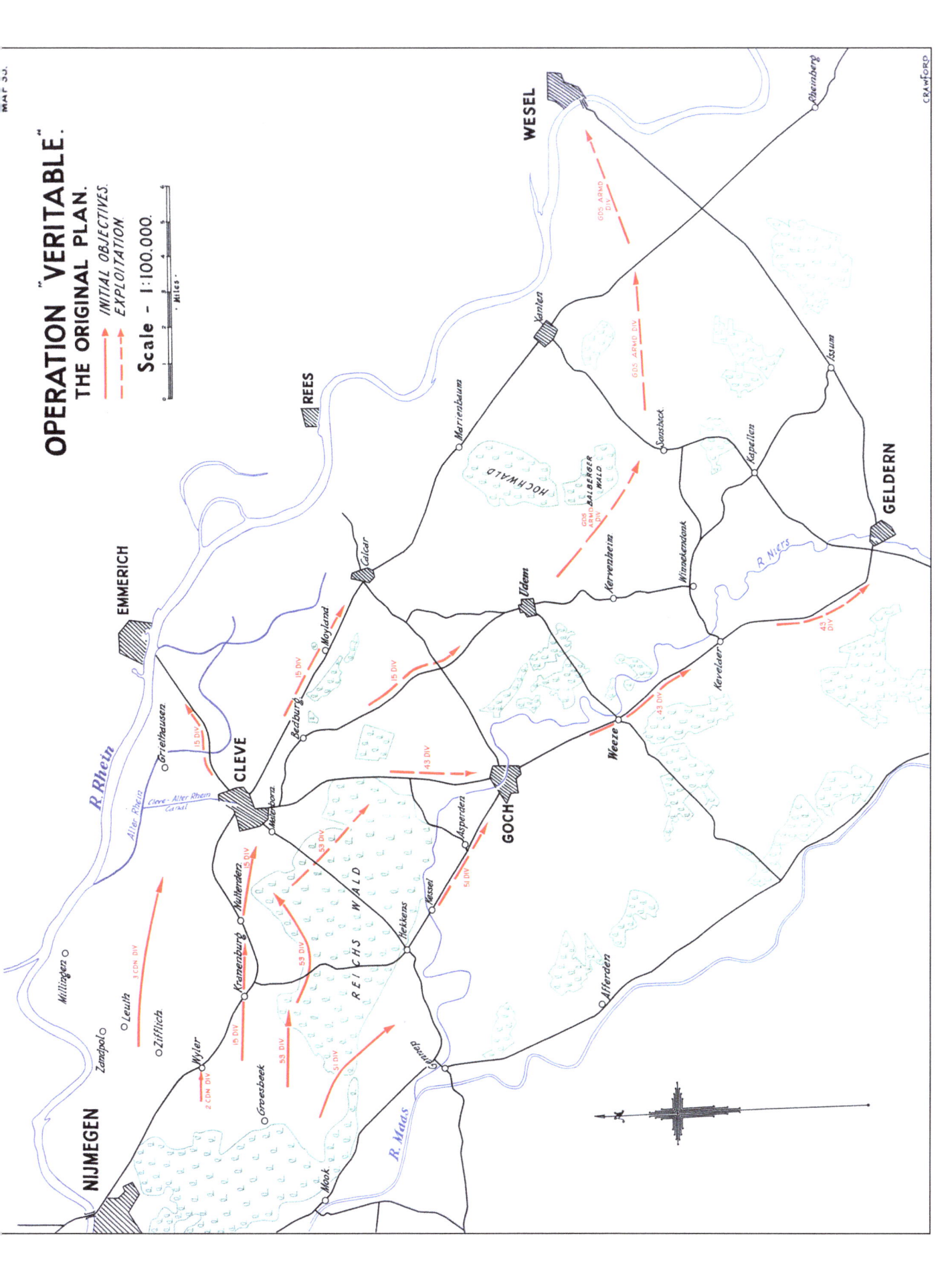

to be defeated. No longer was the success of our divisions to be assessed in ground gained; it was to be counted in the number of German dead that strewed the shellpocked farmlands and in the crowds of prisoners who passed steadily into the Corps cage.

53 (W) Div continued its operations in the southeast corner of the Reichswald and started on the night 13/14 February to take the high ground overlooking Asper bridge. For seventy-two hours, they were involved in almost unceasing fighting of the bitterest type and it was not until the evening of 16 February that their attack secceeded. 51 (H) Div, who now had 32 Guards Brigade under command, captured Kessel on the night 14/15 February and succeeded in bridging the river Niers in front of the town. They then went on to capture Asperden on 16 February, while on their right the Guards took Hommersum, Mull and Hassum.

Meanwhile 130 Inf Brigade of 43 Div had been ordered to advance and take the ridge of high ground running to the southeast of the Cleve Forest; 214 Inf Brigade was to be ready subsequently to pass over this ridge and advance to Goch. The leading battalions of 130 Inf Brigade attacked on 15 February and both gained their objectives; the third battalion attacked the following morning and, in face of very strong opposition, secured the start line for the next attack by 214 Inf Brigade.

The plan of 214 Inf Brigade was to advance with two battalions in a southwesterly direction towards limited objectives and the 5 DCLI (in Kangaroos) and 4 Som L.I. would pass through and secure the escarpment north of Goch*. The attack started at 1500 hrs, 16 February, and after heavy fighting just in front of their start line, the two leading battalions secured their objectives. Then guided by the movement light of searchlights, the armoured column of 5 DCLI, supported by a squadron of 4/7 DG, dashed southwards, and was firm on its objective by 2100 hrs. The attack by 4 Som L.I. went in at 0100 hrs, 17 February, and was a complete success. Later that day, 214 Inf Brigade pushed forward and consolidated on the escarpment overlooking Goch.

These battles by 43 Div may come to be regarded as the turning point of operation Veritable. Since breaking out from Cleve, the division had advanced some ten miles and taken 2,300 prisoners. In spite of a very fierce series of counter-attacks by some of the best enemy

* See Map 38

troops, it had outflanked and rolled up the German lay-back position and the way into Goch from the north was now open.

On 15 February, 2 Canadian Corps took over responsibility for the left of 30 Corps, the boundary running Grave—Groesbeek—Cleve—Udem all inclusive to 2 Cdn Corps. 2* and 3 Cdn Divs reverted to command 2 Cdn Corps and, as had originally been planned, the battle now proceeded on a two Corps front. 52 (L) Div joined 30 Corps on 16 February and took over the right sector of the 51 (H) Div front, with the task of clearing the east bank of the river Maas. Since operation Veritable began more than 7,200 prisoners had been captured and it was estimated that an equal number had been killed or seriously wounded. The measure of defeat inflicted on the enemy at this stage may be assessed by the fact no fewer than eight Panzer Grenadier battalions, thirteen Para battalions and fourteen Infantry battalions had so far been defeated by the Corps.

The Attack on Goch

The next main task for 30 Corps was to capture the important communications centre of Goch, which was heavily defended and was protected by two anti-tank ditches and the R. Niers. The Corps Commander planned that 51 (H) Div should capture the part of the town south of the River and that 43 Div should attack from the escarpment on the north. If determined opposition was encountered, 43 Div was to abandon the frontal assault on the town but was to secure crossings over the first anti-tank ditches and the assault would be put in by 15 (S) Div.

It soon became evident that the enemy was determined to contest Goch and he collected elements of 15 Pz Gr and 8 Para Divs to reinforce 7 Para Div for its defence. Therefore on the night 17/18 February, 214 Inf Brigade was ordered to content itself with making gaps in the anti-tank ditch. The attack on Goch began in earnest on 18 February, 44 Inf Brigade of 15 (S) Div assaulted from the north at 1500 hrs, supported by a crushing artillery programme. By midnight it had reached the outskirts of the town and before daybreak 6 KOSB had bridged the second anti-tank ditch. 51 (H) Div continued their attack from the southwest at 1800 hrs and made good progress troughout the

---

* 2 Cdn Div reverted to command 2nd Cdn Corps after its capture of Wyler.

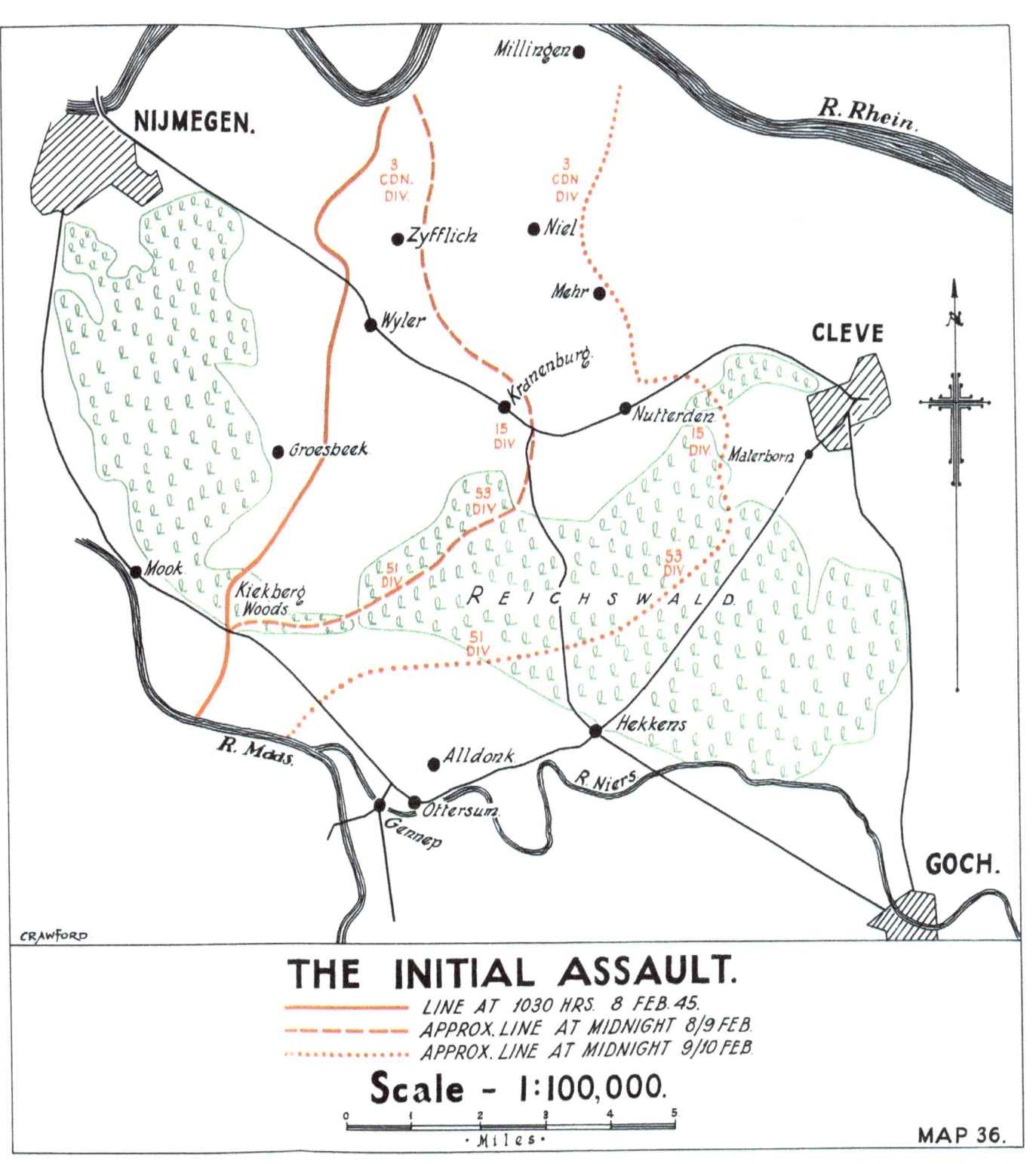

MAP 37

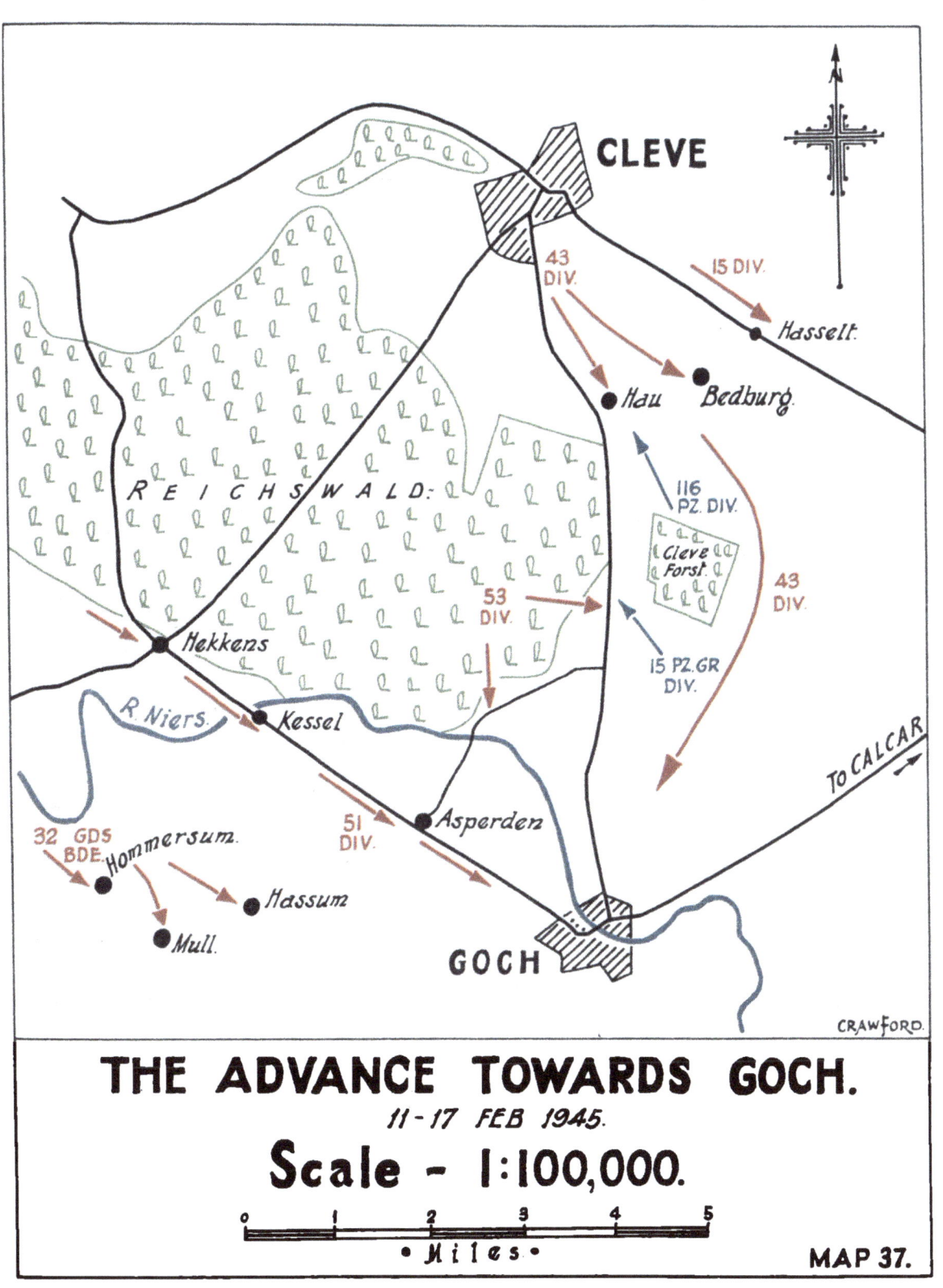

THE ADVANCE TOWARDS GOCH.
11-17 FEB 1945.
Scale - 1:100,000.

MAP 37.

MAP 38

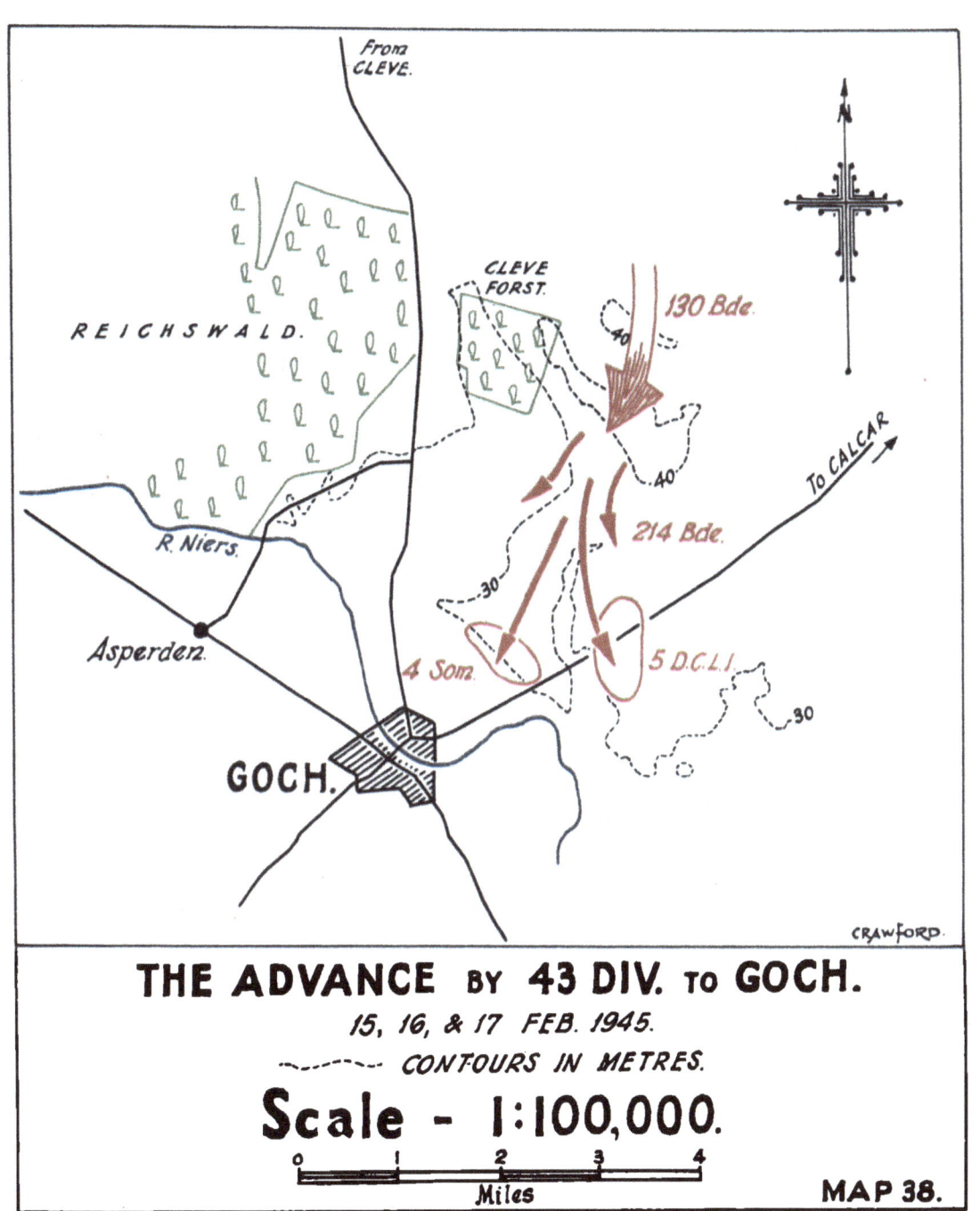

THE ADVANCE BY 43 DIV. TO GOCH.

15, 16, & 17 FEB. 1945.

CONTOURS IN METRES.

Scale - 1:100,000.

MAP 38.

night. During 19 February, as the Scottish divisions drove their way into the town from the northeast and the southwest, the Corps Commander ordered 53 (W) Div to clear the eastern bank of the Niers. By nightfall the whole of the town north of the river had been cleared and over 800 prisoners had been taken. However the effect of the enemy artillery build-up, which was now estimated to amount to some two hundred guns on the Army front, was begining to influence the battle and in the southern parts of Goch, 51 (H) Div was finding progress increasingly difficult. Nevertheless, house-to-house fighting continued day and night without respite, until on the evening of 21 February, Goch could finally be proclaimed clear of the enemy*. 15 (S) Div then continued the advance to the southeast and by 22 February had closed to within 2,500 yards of Weeze.

By this time the total prisoners taken by 30 Corps, in two weeks fighting, exceeded 10,000.

The Battles for Weeze (Map 39)

Blocking the Corps axis, there was now another small defended town, Weeze, which was held by 8 Para Div. 53 (W) Div, which had been given a short rest after the fall of Goch, was ordered to attack and capture Weeze. But before a assault astride the main road into the town could be made, it was necessary to clear a small ridge to the east of the river Niers, which dominated the approach to the town. This task was allotted to 3 Br Div, which had been ordered by the Corps Commander to relieve 15 (S) Div on the Corps left flank.

In spite of heavy opposition from enemy paratroops, 3 Br Div succeeded in clearing the east bank of the Niers. Exceptionally fierce counter-attacks were encountered, especially by a battalion of E Yorks whose leading company had gained a bridgehead over a tributary of the Niers just east of Weeze. One of the most savage battles in the whole operation was fought round this bridgehead.

The attack on Weeze from the north by 53 (W) Div commenced at 0600 hrs on 24 February. The assault was led by two battalions of 160 Inf Brigade, supported by nearly four hundred guns of the Corps artillery and by Flails and Crocodiles of 79 Armd Div. By mid-day, they were astride the Goch — Weeze road about 4,000 yards north of

---

* At this point, 43 Div was withdrawn to rest and refit, in the Cleve area, and subsequently came under command 2 Cdn Corps.

Weeze and during the afternoon they cleared Host. 71 Inf Brigade then started to pass through and, although intense enemy opposition and heavy artillery fire were encountered, it succeeded in getting one company into Rottum. But the impetus of the attack had been slowed and the chances of a breakthrough into the town from the north soon disappeared. Furthermore, the Corps artillery was required to support the Cdn Corps in an operation at this time and so the assault on Weeze was temporarily halted by the Corps Commander's orders at 0515 hrs 25 February.

The offensive by 9 US Army across the river Roer had commenced early on 23 February and striking advances had been made in the first two days. It was good news to 30 Corps to know that the constant move of enemy reinforcements from the southern front would now be halted and that shortly a link-up with its American Allies could be expected. The Canadian operation directed at penetrating the Hochwald "lay-back" and exploiting to Xanten and Wesel commenced on 26 February.

It was natural that the enemy, faced by these threats to his right flank and to his rear, should begin to loosen his hold on the front opposite 30 Corps. But when 53 (W) Div resumed its assault on Weeze on 1 March it found the town still tenaciously defended by 22 Para Regt. However, after 24 hours fighting Weeze was captured and the Welsh division went quickly on to take Kevelaer and Geldern, where it linked up with the Americans. Meanwhile, on the right flank, 52 (L) Div*, reinforced by 1 Commando Brigade, made good progress along the bank of the Maas and by 3 March was holding the general line St Petrusheim — Langstraat — Well.

On the left flank 3 Br Div proceeded to defeat 24 Para Regiment and to capture Kervenheim and Winnekendonk and on 3 March was moving towards Keppelen.

The Advance to Wesel (Map 40)

It had now become evident that the enemy had failed in his efforts to hold the west bank of the Rhine. Realising his defeat, he planned to evacuate as many of his shattered forces as possible through his sole remaining bridgehead at Wesel. All British, Canadian and American forces were therefore directed to liquidate this bridgehead as rapidly as

---

* 52 (L) Div had taken over the whole right sector from 51 (H) Div which was withdrawn to refit.

MAP 39

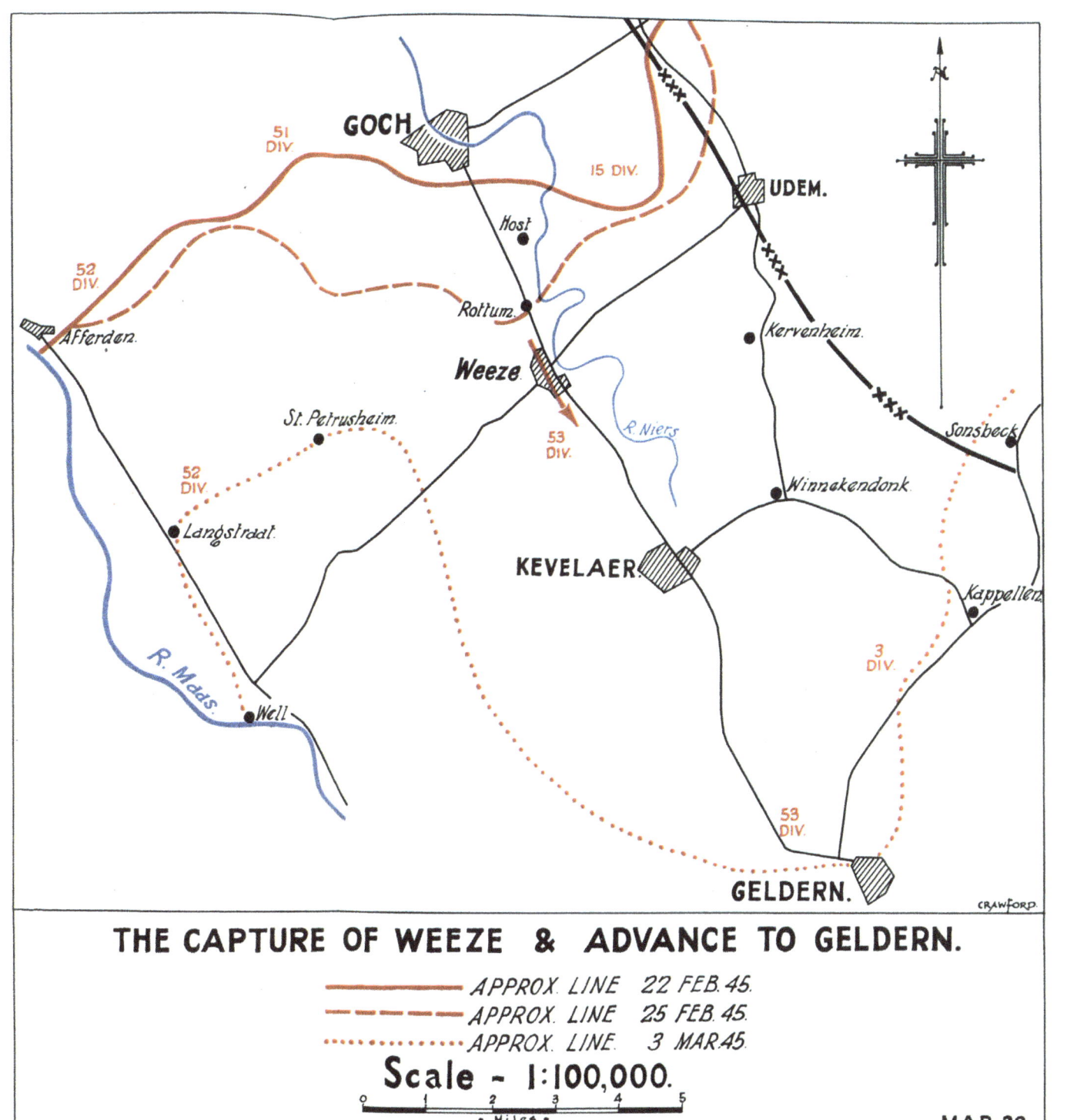

THE CAPTURE OF WEEZE & ADVANCE TO GELDERN.

—— APPROX. LINE 22 FEB. 45.
– – – APPROX. LINE 25 FEB. 45.
· · · · APPROX. LINE 3 MAR. 45.

Scale – 1:100,000.

MAP 39.

possible. 30 Corps advanced on a two divisional front with 53 (W) Div right and 3 Br Div left; 52 (L) Div had now been "pinched out" by the approach of the Americans to Geldern. 53 (W) Div captured Issum on 4 March but met increasingly heavy opposition on approaching the wooded country south of Alpen and did not succeed in clearing this area until 7 March. 3 Br Div captured Kappelen and, in spite of the inevitable delay caused by demolitions, cleared the Winkelscher Busch and made contact with 3 Cdn Div on the left. Guards Armd Div, which was pushed through 3 Br Div on 4 March, then advanced eastwards and captured Bonninghardt. 52 (L) Div now relieved 53 (W) Div on the Corps right flank and, in the face of heavy shelling, captured Alpen.

At 1800 hrs, 8 March, with the liquidation of the Wesel bridgehead in sight*, operational command of all troops under 30 Corps passed to 2 Cdn Corps. Thus ended 30 Corps' part in the destruction of the German Army west of the Rhine. During the course of the battle nine British and Canadian divisions, supported by a vast array of artillery, had been under command of the Corps, and neither a day or night had passed since 8 February without at least one formation being engaged in the attack. In spite of all the difficulties normally attendant upon winter fighting in the flood-plains of northwestern Europe, the Corps had succeeded in penetrating the most carefully prepared defensive positions of the enemy, and had encountered and defeated or disorganised no less than three Panzer divisions, four Para divisions and four infantry divisions. More than 16,800 prisoners had been captured and it was estimated that about 7,000 of the enemy had been killed or seriously wounded.

The western bank of the Rhine, springboard to the heart of Germany had been made secure.

---

* The enemy evacuated the bridgehead completely on the night 9/10 March.

MAP 40

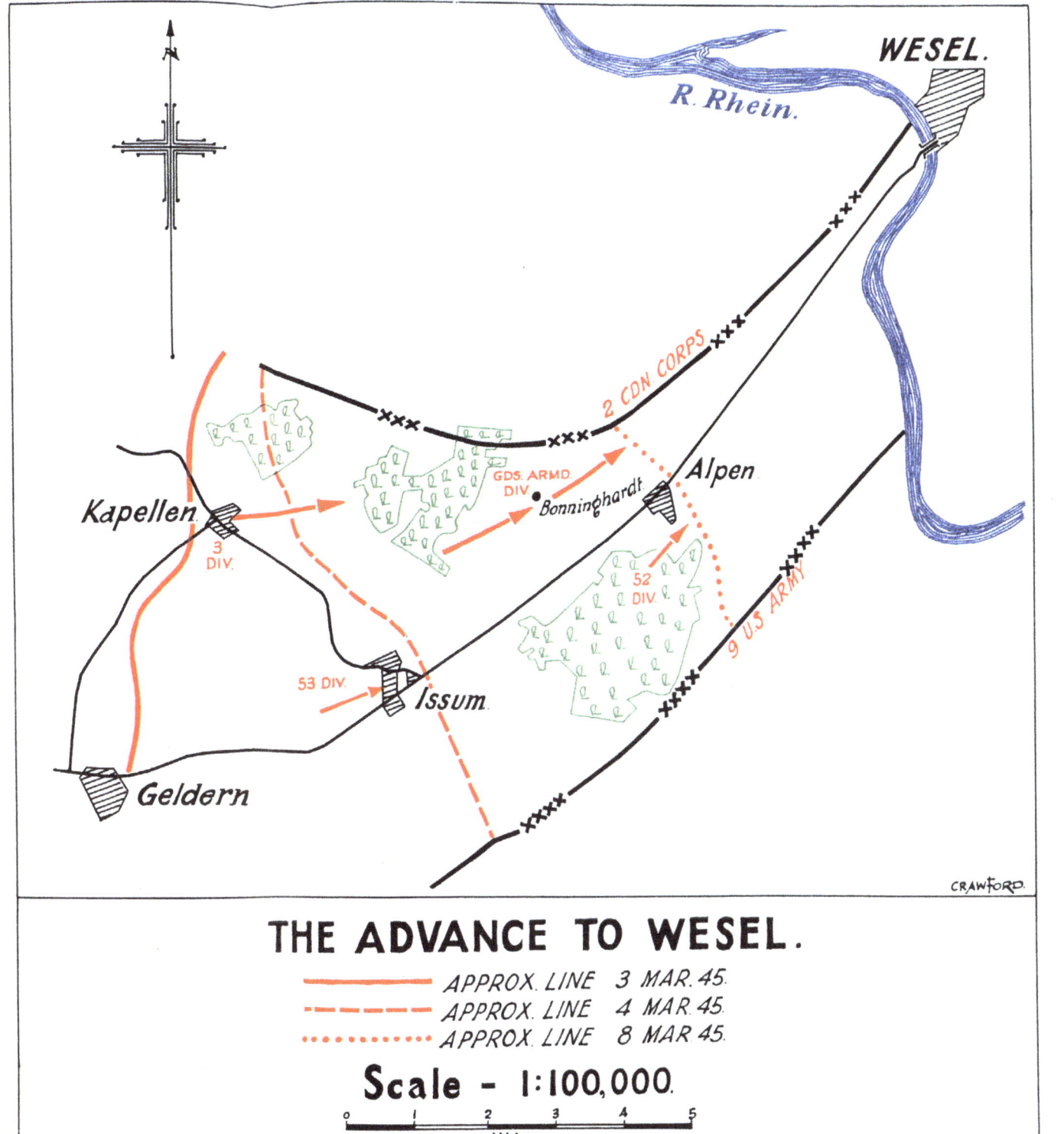

THE ADVANCE TO WESEL.

― APPROX. LINE 3 MAR. 45.
--- APPROX. LINE 4 MAR. 45.
··· APPROX. LINE 8 MAR. 45.

Scale - 1:100,000.

MAP 40.

CHAPTER SEVEN

Across the Rhine and into Germany

The crossing of the Rhine — 23 March 1945

No sooner had operation Veritable been completed with the clearance of the enemy bridgehead west of Wesel, than 30 Corps was instructed to plan their part in operation Plunder — the crossing of the river Rhine.

Second Army (consisting of 2 Cdn, 8, 12, and 30 Corps) was to cross the Rhine on a two Corps front between incl Wesel — excl Emmerich, with right 12 Corps and left 30 Corps*. The intention of the 30 Corps Commander was to capture Rees and Haldern and to establish a bridgehead sufficiently deep to permit bridges to be built, preparatory to a further advance into Germany. He ordered 51 (H) Div, with under command one brigade of 3 Cdn Div, to make the assault and secure the initial bridgehead.

It was known that the enemy forces which would oppose the Corps once again largely consisted of paratroops. 8 Para Div was deployed in the area of Rees with parts of 6 and 7 Para Divs on the flanks. In immediate reserve were 15 Pz Gr Div and 116 Pz Div. In addition, an unusually high proportion of enemy guns, estimated to amount to 150 pieces, was covering the Corps front.

All movement into the confined concentration area, in the open farm land of the lower Rhine valley, was carried out in darkness. The task of moving guns and ammunition, infantry and tanks, and a great quantity of bridging material into this small area demanded a high degree of organisation and a careful regard to camouflage.

---

* 30 Corps Order of Battle, Appendix "E".

The prelude to the Corps attack was opened at 1700 hrs on 23 March 45 by the Corps artillery. The bombardment was designed firstly to destroy the enemy batteries and later, increasing in intensity, to neutralise the enemy infantry. Then at 2100 hrs, in the hazy darkness of a warm spring evening, the leading "Buffaloes" of 30 Armd Brigade, carrying infantry of 153 and 154 Inf Brigades, slid into the Rhine. Upstream at Wesel, aircraft of Bomber Command could be heard preparing the way for 12 Corps which was to assault later that night. At four minutes past nine, the Corps Commander received a signal at his OP that the first British troops to cross the Rhine — men of the Black Watch — had safely landed on the enemy bank. The river crossing proceeded smoothly during the night; opposition was not so heavy as might have been expected and casualties were not large. But the enemy was quick to recover and desperately defended the town of Rees; within 24 hours of the assault, he committed 15 Pz Gr Div against 30 Corps.

Fighting was particularly fierce, especially at the main exits from the town, where battle groups of the Panzer Grenadiers quickly staged determined counter attacks. The ferocity of the fighting at this stage can be illustrated by the following account of a gallant action fought by 1 Battalion, Black Watch:—

> The village of Speldrop had been captured on the night of 23/24 March and soon afterwards was counter attacked by infantry and SP guns. The position became extremely confused and Lieutenant J. R. Henderson, the Black Watch (RHR), knowing that the holding of the village, which lay astride the main Rees—Emmerich road, was vital to the development of the Rhine bridgehead, volunteered to lead a patrol to find the exact extent of the enemy penetration. From the outset the patrol came under intense MG fire and, as heavy casualties were being sustained, Lieutenant Henderson ordered the rest of the patrol to take cover while he and a Bren gunner went forward alone.
>
> Almost immediately an enemy machine gun opened fire at very close range; the Bren gunner was killed and the officer's revolver was knocked out of his hand. Seizing his shovel Lieutenant Henderson charged the machine gun position

alone and killed the gunner with his shovel. He then made his way back to his patrol, and although the only building at hand was already in flames he got his men into it and put it into a state of defence. By this time, the officer and his patrol were completely cut off from the rest of the battalion and all attempts to gain contact with them were unsuccessful. In the meantime, Lieutenant Henderson, realising that his small party had no LMG, crawled forward a distance of 60 yards, under very heavy, close range fire, to where the Bren gunner had been killed, collected the Bren gun and with great difficulty made his way back to his men. Armed with this weapon, the beleaguered patrol held out for over 12 hours against all attempts to dislodge them. During the whole of this time the enemy's attacks against the house never relaxed and on six separate occasions these attacks were supported by Bazookas fired at short range. Thus were the efforts of the enemy to advance further towards Rees in the sector frustrated.

The bridgehead was gradually extended by 51 (H) Div. Within forty eight hours of the first crossing, the important factory area north of Rees had been cleared and 9 Cdn Inf Brigade (under command 51 (H) Div) had reached the outskirts of Bienen. On 26 March*, 1 Gordons were able to report that all enemy in Rees had been eliminated, 43 Div cleared Millingen and 9 Cdn Inf Brigade captured Bienen. An attack was also made by 51 Div towards Isselberg, as a result of which the important bridge on the main exit from Rees was captured intact.

It was now the Corps Commander's intention to get each division on a narrow front, so that it would be possible to attack the enemy continuously both by day and night. 3 Br Div therefore crossed the Rhine on 27 March and took over part of the right sector of the bridgehead from 51 (H) Div, and 3 Cdn Div took over the extreme left sector from 43 Div.

On 28 March gains were made all along the perimeter of the bridgehead. 3 Br Div entered Haldern, 51 (H) Div captured Isselburg and 43 Div captured Megchelen. At 1200 hrs, 3 Cdn Div, which had just taken Dornick and Vrasselt, passed to command 2 Cdn Corps.

---

* At 2359 hrs, 25 March, 43 Div assumed command of the left sector of the bridgehead and 9 Cdn Inf Brigade passed to command 43 Div.

Further gains were made as a result of heavy fighting on 29 March. 3 Br Div captured Werth and 43 Div took Anholt and secured crossings over the stream north of the town.

Meanwhile the Sappers had been building the ferries and bridges. Within two hours of the beginning of the assault, storm boats had been made ready to ferry infantry across the river and by daybreak, in spite of casualties from enemy fire, four battalions were safely carried over in addition to those which had gone across in "Buffaloes". Throughout the night preparations to build rafts and bridges had continued under sporadic shell and mortar fire. Unfortunately owing to the failure completely to clear the northern waterfront, the vast scene of Sapper activity on the south bank was revealed to enemy observers in Rees, as soon as the morning mist lifted from the river. However although any movement on the ferry sites brought down accurate observed fire, work on the rafts continued and by 1900 hrs, 24 March, three rafts had started ferrying opposite Rees. The other ferry site, further downstream, had better luck and many tanks and other vehicles were safely carried across.

The first bridge, which was christened Waterloo Bridge, (a Class 9, FBE), was completed at 0100 hrs 26 March, and Lambeth Bridge (a Class 15, Bailey) was opened at 0830 hrs, the same day. Meanwhile, work on the Class 40 bridges proceeded apace and first London bridge was completed at midnight 26/27 March, then Blackfriars at noon on 28 March and finally Westminster in the evening of 29 March. The latter was officially opened by General Sir Miles Dempsey, Commander Second Army, who told a gathering of Sappers that the Rhine battle was now won and that the RE, by building the bridges across this great river, had done their part to allow the armour to cross and tear the heart out of Germany. In the completion of this work, 155 all ranks had been killed or wounded.

The breakout from the Bridgehead (Map 42)

The next task of 30 Corps was to advance deep into Germany, protecting the left flank of Second Army. Guards Armd Div was accordingly directed to advance on the axis Groenlo—Enschede—Emsburen—Quakenbruck—Bremen—Hamburg. 43 Div was to provide

MAP 41

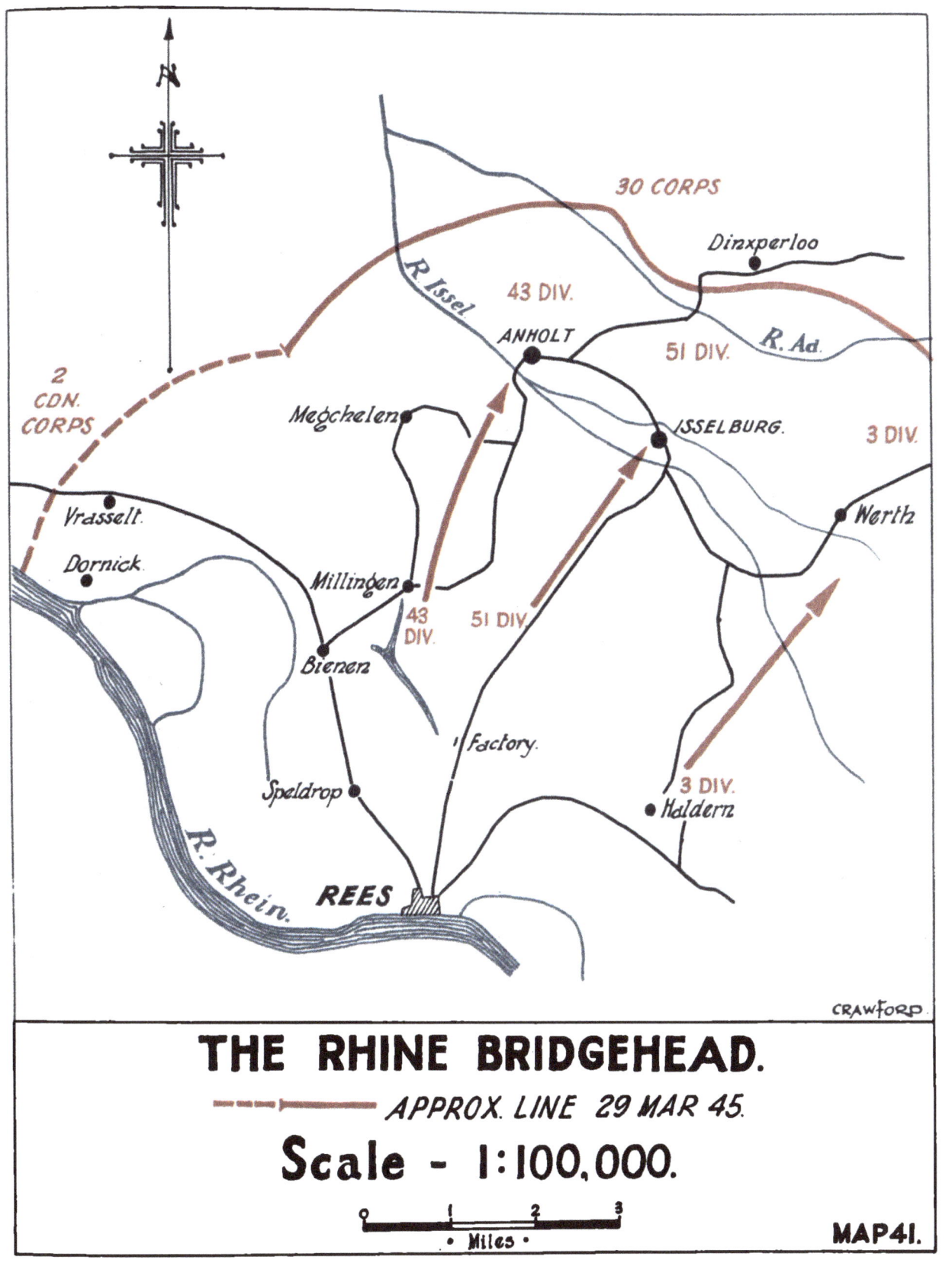

THE RHINE BRIDGEHEAD.
APPROX. LINE 29 MAR 45.
Scale - 1:100,000.

left flank protection for the Corps and 3 Div was to follow Guards Armd Div as an immediate Corps reserve. 51 Div was to rest in the Rees—Isselburg area.

The Guards Armd Div passed through 51 (H) Div on 30 March and, overcoming many demolitions on its axis, captured Aalten. On the left, 43 Div with 8 Armd Brigade leading their advance, pushed about four miles north of Anholt. Throughout the next few days steady advances were made. Progress however was not rapid because most stubborn resistance was offered continuously by determined paratroops, skilfully commanded by 2 Para Corps. This formation managed to exercise a high degree of control throughout the withdrawal and its demolition of both roads and bridges was most thorough.

Groenlo and Enschede were captured by the Guards Armd Div and by 2 April, it had reached Nordhorn and Bentheim. On the left, 43 Div had cleared Ruurlo and was preparing to attack Hengelo from the east. 3 Br Div, moving behind the Guards, had occupied Enschede.

Some fifteen miles ahead of the Guards Armd Div there now lay the river Ems and the Dortmund—Ems Canal, which converged near Lingen. The passage of these formidable obstacles was certain to be heavily contested as, by this time, the defeated enemy para divs had been reinforced by a miscellaneous collection of Wehrkreis units and the Grossdeutschland Training Brigade. The Commander of the Guards Armd Div therefore decided to make an audacious attempt to "bounce" the Lingen bridges, with a combined group of Scots and Welsh Guards. Accordingly, just before midnight on 2 April, the Scots Guards climbed on to the Cromwell tanks of the Welsh Guards and set off at full speed down the main road out of Nordhorn. During this wild dash, German SPs and transport and Germans on foot were encountered. Throughout the dark journey, the tanks opened fire on everything that even looked like a target and inflicted heavy casualties on the enemy both in men and material. Approaching the first bridge at Lingen, the infantry dismounted and two platoons rushed across the river. But no sooner had they reached the far bank, than the enemy blew the bridge and thus frustrated the final coup of a gallant effort, which deserved greater success.

The next day, the Coldstream Guards wrought vengeance. At first light patrols of 2 HCR reported that the bridge just north of Lingen was intact and still in use by the enemy. A company group of tanks and infantry was immediately directed to capture this bridge (Map 43). Preliminary reconnaissance revealed that it was covered by entrenched enemy infantry and 88 mm guns and was prepared for demolition with 500 lb bombs. As the leading platoons, who were covered by fire from their supporting tanks, approached the bridge, the enemy reaction became most violent. Capt I. O. Liddell, Coldstream Guards, thereupon ordered his company to halt and ran alone to the bridge. He scaled the ten foot high road block guarding it and then, in the face of point blank fire, succeeded in cutting the wires to each of the 500 lb demolition bombs. His task accomplished he recrossed the bridge and, standing on the road block in full view of the enemy, signalled the leading platoons to advance. Inspired by his example, they charged the bridge and captured or killed its garrison of one hundred Germans. Three 88 mm guns and two 20 mm guns, which had been firing throughout the action, were captured and the bridge was taken intact*.

Meanwhile, 185 Inf Brigade, of 3 Br Div, had been reconnoitring the canal and river south of Lingen, prior to making an assault crossing there that night. But as soon as it became known that the Coldstream Guards had captured the northern river bridge intact, the Commander of 185 Inf Brigade changed his plan and, even though no reconnaissance would be possible, he decided to make his crossing in that area. The Brigade accordingly formed up, crossed the Coldstream bridge, and assaulted the canal, which was stubbornly defended by the enemy. The successful completion of this operation in the dark, without previous reconnaissance, was no mean achievement.

There then followed 48 hours stiff fighting with 3 Br Div opposed by two battle groups — 7 Para Div and the Grossdeutschland Training Brigade — before Lingen was captured. 3 Br Div then moved southwards on the far bank of the canal, thus opening another crossing about five miles south of Lingen and establishing contact with 51 Div, which had moved forward on the right flank from Enschede.

The approach to Bremen (Map 44)

With the clearance of Lingen by 3 Br Div, the Corps advance was continued with Guards Armd Div directed to the east and 43 Div, which had now been brought forward, directed to the northeast. Guards Armd

---

* Captain Liddell, who was later killed in action, was awarded the Victoria Cross for his gallantry that day.

MAP 42

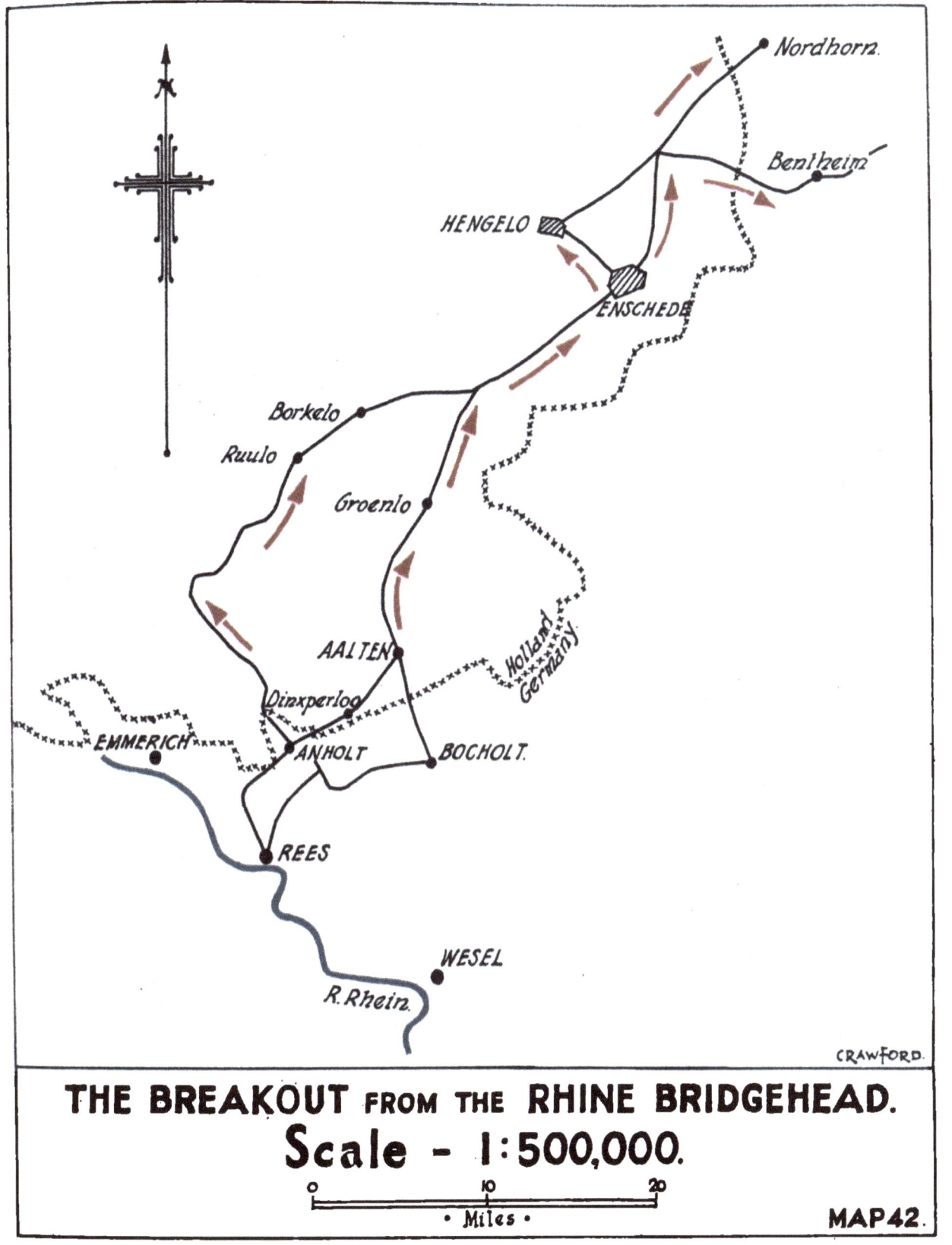

THE BREAKOUT FROM THE RHINE BRIDGEHEAD.
Scale - 1:500,000.

MAP 42.

MAP 43

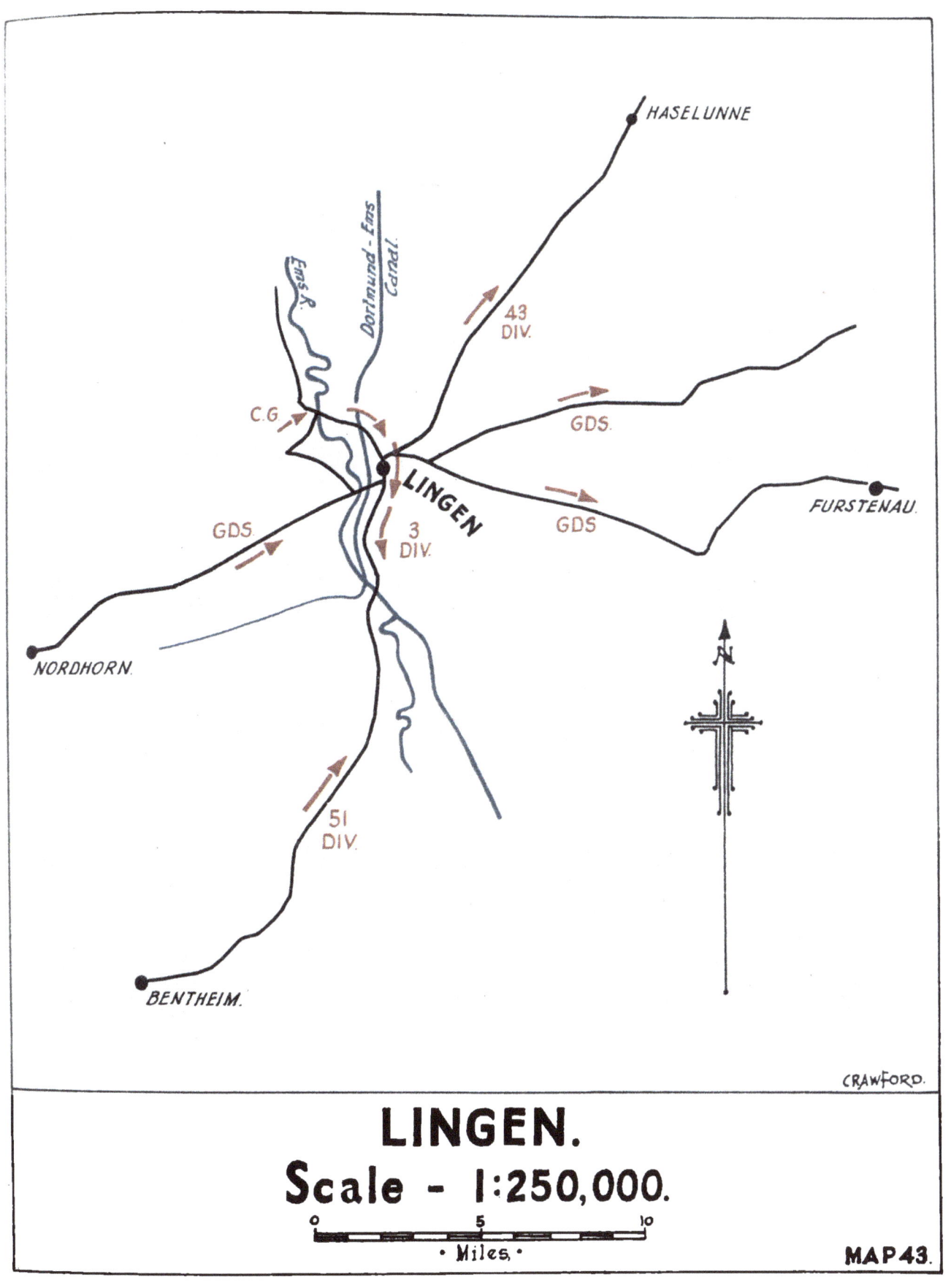

LINGEN.
Scale - 1:250,000.

Div started their advance on 6 April and covered about five miles that day. On 7 April the Guards overcame strong opposition and started to attack Freren; 43 Div passed through Lingen and moved towards Haselunne.

The advance continued steadily for the next few days but progress was not fast, owing to the determined resistance of the enemy paratroops and to the extremely thorough demolition of bridges and cratering of roads. By 10 April, Guards Armd Div had reached Bippen and Menslage whilst on the north 43 Div had secured crossings over the river Hase and had cleared Haselunne. On this date, 3 Br Div passed to command 12 Corps and moved out of the 30 Corps sector.

On 11 April, the Corps Commander ordered 51 (H) Div to advance on the southernmost axis and the Corps now moved forward with all three divs up; 51 (H) Div right, Guards Armd Div centre, 43 Div left. Progress was still hampered by demolitions, road blocks and mines, invariably covered by determined rearguards. By 13 April, 43 Div had entered Cloppenburg capturing its bridge intact and the Guards Armd Div had reached Emstek. In the south, 51 Div had captured Hanstedt.

The main weight of the Second Army thrust was now diverted northeastwards, 8 Corps being directed on Lubeck and 12 Corps on Hamburg. The role of 30 Corps was now, still carrying out its task of left flank protection for the Second Army, to mask Bremen from the south and southwest. 3 Br Div, which was located in the Wildeshausen — Harpstedt area reverted to command 30 Corps and was given the task of capturing Brinkum and Delmenhorst. Their left flank was protected by 51 (H) Div. Guards Armd Div was withdrawn and placed under command 12 Corps and the front of 43 Div, on the Corps extreme left flank was gradually taken over by 2 Cdn Corps.

The Corps bag of prisoners since the crossing of the Rhine now exceeded 10,000.

The capture of Bremen (Map 45)

The majority of the Para Army now withdrew northwards to the Emden — Wilhelmshaven peninsula, while HQ 2 Para Corps withdrew to Bremen. However, the advance of 3 Br Div was not unopposed and two "ersatz" divisions of the Wehrkreis — 471 and 490 — were encountered and destroyed; the bag of prisoners on 14 April alone amounting to no less than 1,200. The fighting was particularly bitter in Brinkum, where fanatical youths of the SS Training Battalions, well led by competent NCOs, fought stubbornly in house to house fighting. Brinkum was finally cleared on 17 April and Delmenhorst on 19 April. Thus 30 Corps closed with Bremen from the southwest.

On 19 April, 52 (L) Div, which had crossed the Weser with 12 Corps, came under command 30 Corps. Plans were now made for the capture of Bremen. The Corps Commander intended to take the city by two main thrusts: —

(a) <u>North of river Weser</u> by 43 Div right and 52 Div left.

(b) <u>South of river Weser</u> by 3 Br Div with a feint attack by 51 Div.

Throughout the period 19—23 April, 52 (L) Div continued relentlessly to close on the city. It encountered very strong opposition to the east of Bremen but succeeded in capturing Achim and the high ground to the north on 22 April. Meanwhile 43 Div was moved across the river Weser and came into contact with the enemy on the right of 52 (L) Div.

The main assault on Bremen commenced on 24 April. 52 (L) Div, attacking along the north bank of the Weser, broke into Arbergen and thus penetrated the main eastern defences of the city. On the following day, it continued its advance and pushed right into the city, capturing well over a thousand prisoners. 3 Br Div, on the left bank of the river, reached Kattenturm during the night 24/25 April and then advanced across the ruins of the Focke-Wulfe factory to penetrate deep into the southern outskirts of the city, capturing another 1,000 prisoners. On the right flank 43 Div reached the autobahn. By midnight on 26 April, it could be said that Bremen, the first big German port on the North Sea to fall to the Allies, had been captured by 30 Corps. In the last four days, 6,000 prisoners (including two generals and one admiral) had been captured by the Corps.

<u>The Last Battles (Map 46)</u>

After the capture of Bremen, 30 Corps was ordered to clear the peninsula which lies between the estuaries of the Elbe and the Weser. Much of the country in the peninsula was marshy and few of the roads

MAP 44

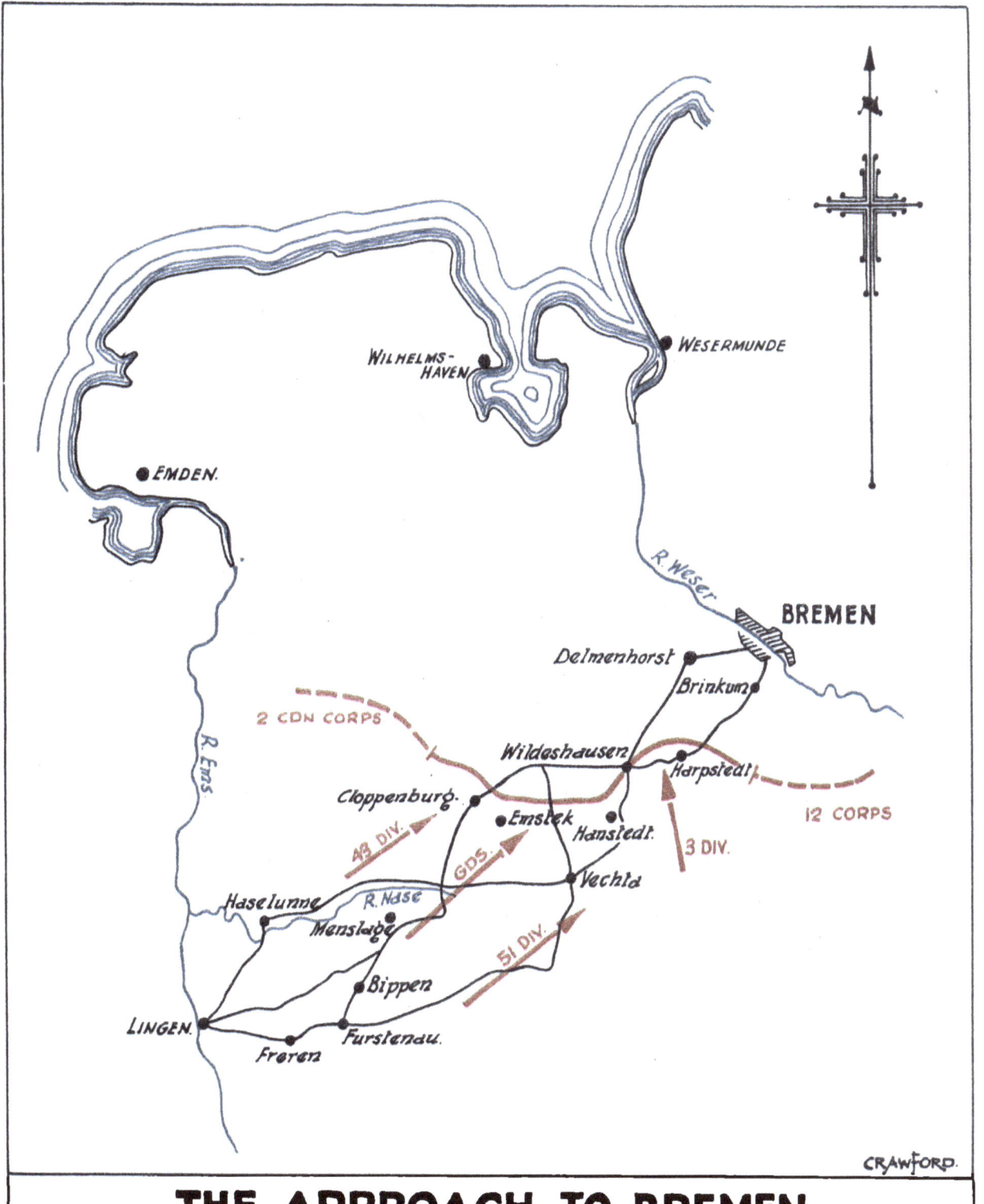

THE APPROACH TO BREMEN.

---- APPROX. LINE AT 13 APRIL 1945.

Scale - 1:1,000,000.

MAP 44.

MAP 45

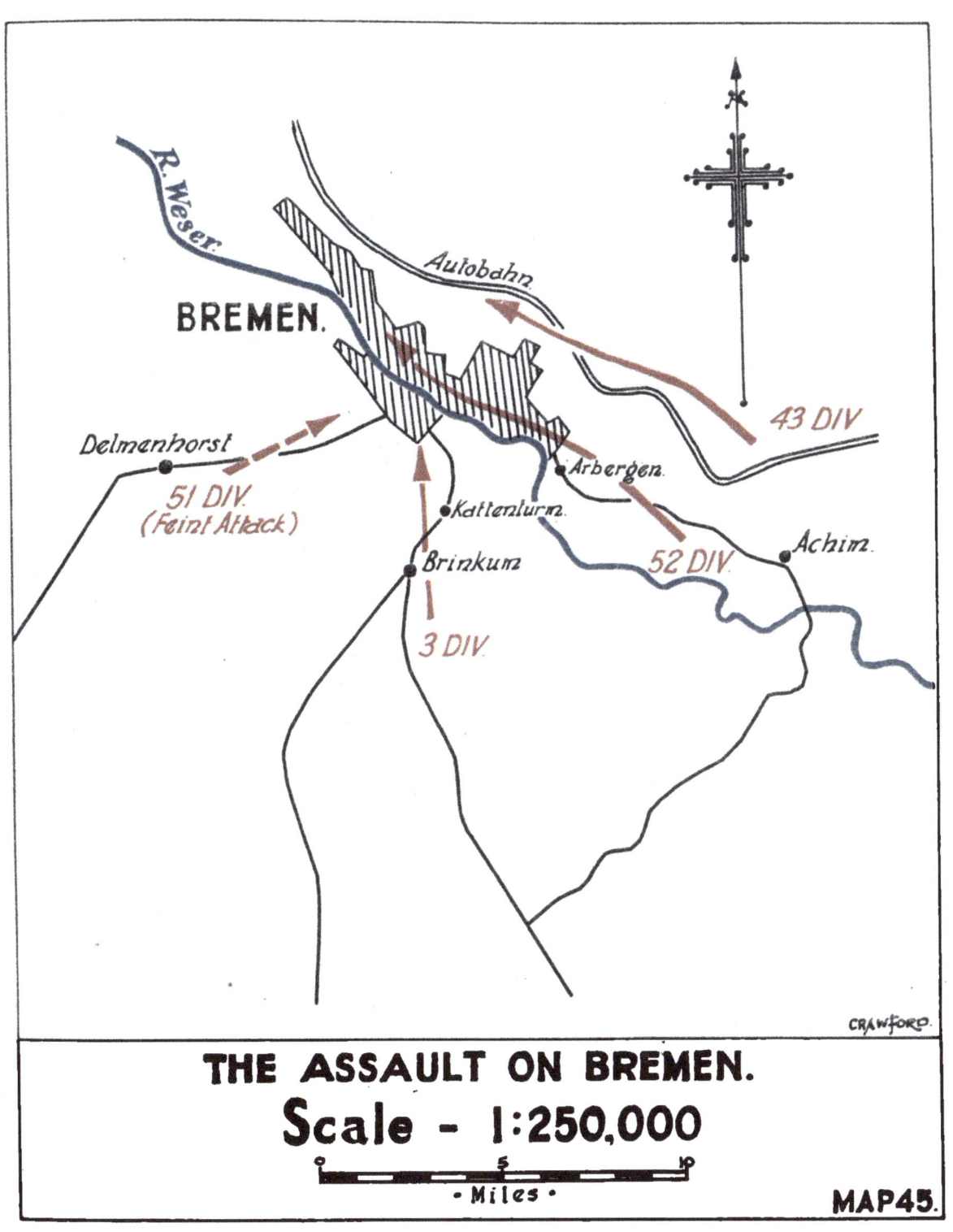

THE ASSAULT ON BREMEN.
Scale - 1:250,000

MAP 45.

were good. The enemy extensively used bombs and sea mines for cratering the roads and, on this account, progress was never rapid. 51 (H) Div crossed the Weser and coming into the line on the right of 43 Div, was directed to advance northeastwards from Bremen. 43 Div was to advance due north up the Hamme valley, whilst 52 (L) Div pushed westwards through Bremen.

51 (H) Div started its advance from the outskirts of Bremen on 27 April and within 48 hours had pushed about six miles north along the Autobahn. 43 Div, on the left, contacted the enemy at Quelkhorn on 28 April.

On 29 April, Guards Armd Div reverted to command 30 Corps from 12 Corps. At this time the division was pressing towards Bremervorde and had a recce screen extending some twelve miles to the east. The Guards were now directed to protect the northern flank of the Corps and pushed a brigade group out towards Stade. Meanwhile 51 (H) Div was making good progress northwards and linked up with the Guards outside Bremervorde on 30 April. 43 Div was methodically clearing pockets of enemy from the water meadows on the east bank of the Hamme river.

The Guards Armd Div negotiated the surrender of Stade on 1 May and immediately occupied the town. To the south, 43 Div was ordered to make an assault crossing of the Hamme but was severely delayed by the appalling cratering of all the approach roads. On the night of 1/2 May, 51 (H) Div crossed the river to the east of Bremervorde and captured the German garrison of 300 in the town. In the extreme south, 52 (L) Div now relieved of most of its responsibilities in Bremen crossed the river Wumme and commenced to relieve 214 Inf Brigade of 43 Div in the marshlands.

Rumours regarding a German request for an armistice were now becoming current throughout the Corps. In fact, the Corps Commander received news of the German negotiations on 3 May, but this information could not be passed on to formations. In order to save lives, however, he found excuses to order each division to slacken the tempo of its advance. The Guards Armd Div and 51 (H) Div made good progress this day in their westward drives, the former from Stade and the latter from Bremervorde. 43 Div closed up to the river Hamme.

On 4 May, all divisions continued their advances. A patrol of 2 Derby Yeomanry, on 51 (H) Div front, received a request from 15 Pz Gr Div to open negotiations for the surrender of the whole division. These negotiations were still in progress when news of the impending surrender of all enemy forces on 21 Army Group front came through. At about 2030 hrs, on 4 May, a signal was received that all hostilities would cease at 0800 hrs the following morning. All troops stood firm and no further fighting occurred.

At 1100 hrs, on 5 May, the German commanders of Corps Ems and 15 Pz Gr Div were given orders regarding their surrender by the B.G.S. At 1430 hrs that day the Corps Commander gave his personal orders to the German Corps Commander.

Thus ended for 30 Corps its long journey to Victory, which had commenced at Alamein in Africa, some three years earlier. During its last campaign, it had travelled from the beaches of Normandy across the length of Europe and in this time all formations of the British Second Army and three American divisions had served with it. If, when the larger histories of this war are written, any credit is accorded to 30 Corps for its achievements, it will be due to the fighting soldiers of all those divisions, whose deeds are so inadequately described in this volume, but, who all did their part in carrying the signs of "Club Route" to its rightful end in Germany.

MAP 46

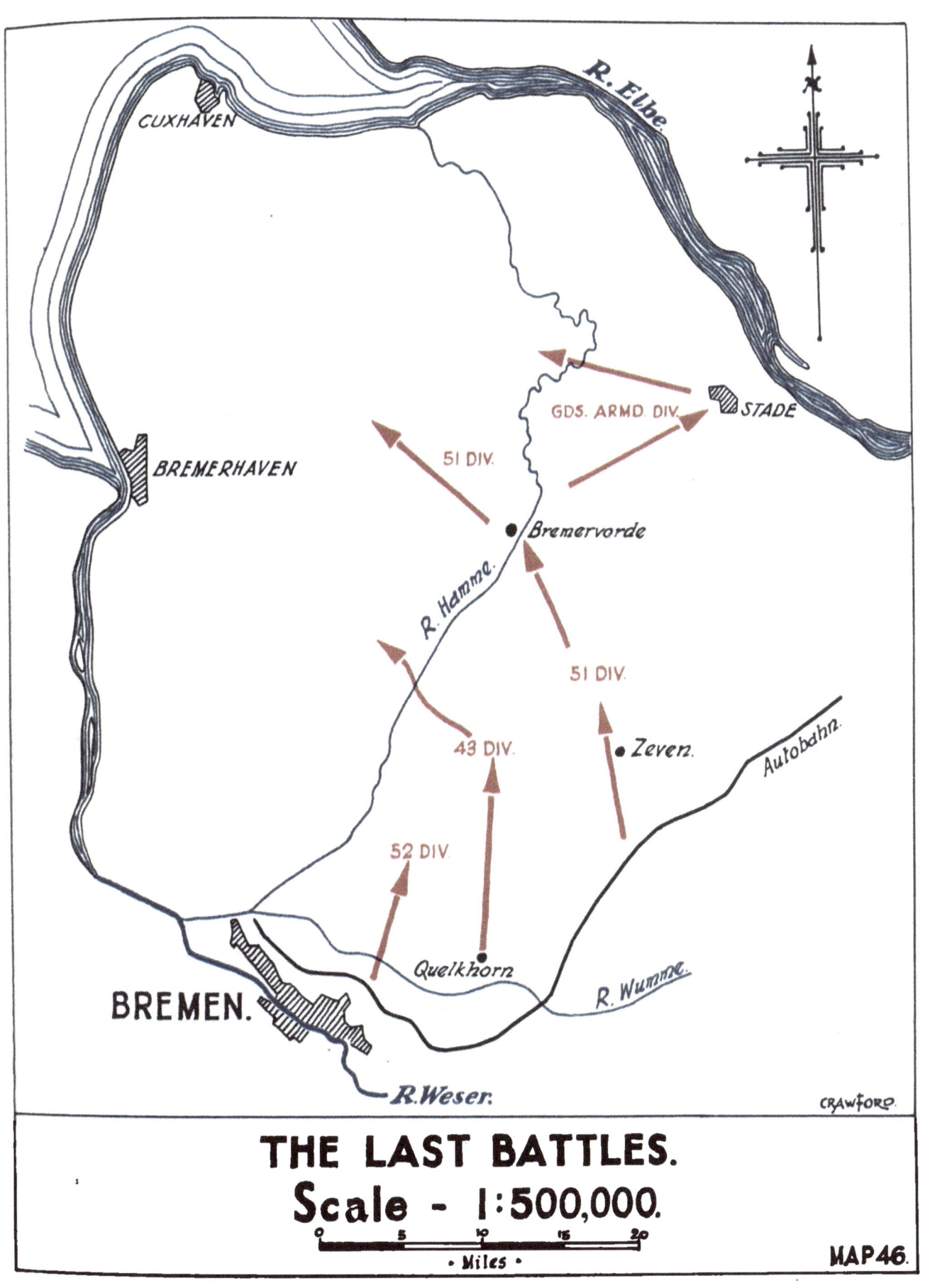

THE LAST BATTLES.
Scale - 1:500,000.

MAP 46.

Appendix "A"

Operation Overlord
30 Corps Order of Battle

7 Armd Div
    7 Armd Div
    64 Med Regt RA

49 Inf Div
    49 Inf Div
    33 Armd Bde
    121 Med Regt RA

50 (N) Div
    50 (N) Div
    56 Inf Bde
    8 Armd Bde
        Two Sqns, Westminster Dgns
        Det 141 RAC
    987 Bn US Arty (155 mm SP)
    86 and 147 Fd Regts RA
      7 Med Regt RA
        Two btys, 73 A tk Regt RA
      6 Assault Regt RE
      47 (RM) Commando

Appendix "B"

Operation "Market Garden"
Outline Order of Battle

1. <u>30 Corps</u>
    - 101 US Airborne Div
    - Guards Armd Div
    - 43 (W) Div
    - 50 (N) Div
    - 8 Armd Bde
    - 86 and 147 Fd Regts RA
    - 7, 64 and 84 Med Regts RA
    - 419/52 Hy Bty RA
    - 100 AA Bde
    - 7 Army Tps RE

2. <u>British Airborne Corps</u>
    - 1 Br Airborne Div
    - 82 US Airborne Div (subsequently passed to command 30 Corps)
    - Polish Para Bde

Appendix "C"

Operation Veritable

30 Corps Outline Order of Battle for the Assault

    2 HCR
    6 Gds Armd Brigade
    8 Armd Brigade
    34 Armd Brigade
        Eleven regts of 79 Armd Div
        Two APC Regts (Kangaroos)

RA
    3, 4, 5 and 9 AGRAs
    2 Cdn AGRA
        Two SL Btys RA
        Two AOP Sqns
    1 Cdn Rocket Unit
    106 AA Bde

RE
    6 Assault Regt RE
    42 Assault Regt RE

Divs
    Guards Armd Div
    15 (S) Div
    43 (W) Div
    51 (H) Div
    53 (W) Div
        2 Cdn Div (one brigade only)
        3 Cdn Div

Appendix "D"

Operation Veritable

Outline Artillery Fire Plan: D Day

(a) No firing before 0500 hrs D Day except by 2 and 3 Cdn Divs.

(b) 0500—0945 hrs
   (i) Harassing of enemy HQs and communications,
   (ii) Bombardment of enemy locations to destroy as many enemy as possible and utterly demoralise the survivors,
   (iii) Deception smoke screens,
   (iv) Counter battery and counter mortar.

(c) 0945—1600 hrs
   (i) Barrage in support of attack by 2 Cdn Div, 15 (S) Div and 53 (W) Div, see Note 2.
   (ii) Concentrations and "Stonks" in support of attack by 51 (H) Div,
   (iii) Smoke screens,
   (iv) Bombardment of enemy localities in depth.

(d) 1700—2100 hrs
   (i) Support of 3 Cdn Div attack,
   (ii) Preparation for 15 (S) and 53 (W) Divs' second attack.

(e) 2100—0100 hrs
   (i) Support of second attacks by 15 (S) and 53 (W) Divs,
   (ii) Preparation for 15 (S) Div final attack.

(f) 0100—0900 hrs
   Support of 15 (S) Div final attack.

Notes:
1. Throughout the whole of D Day, when well over 500,000 rounds were fired, not one single case was reported of a round falling short amongst our own troops.
2. There were several interesting features of the barrage. The fire was arranged always to cover a depth of 500 yards, by means of

fire lines at 100 yards intervals. Each line was moved forward 300 yards every twelve minutes. One minute before the end of firing on each block, all guns on the front line ceased firing high explosive. One gun per troop then immediately fired a round of yellow smoke as an indication to the infantry that no more high explosive would be fired on that line and that the barrage would lift in one minute.

Appendix "E"

Operation Plunder

30 Corps Outline Order of Battle

RAC
- Royals
- Inns of Court
- Staffs Yeo
- 8 Armd Bde
- 30 Armd Bde (in support)

RA
- 4 AGRA
- 5 AGRA
- 106 AA Bde

RE
- 13 AGRE

Divs
- Guards Armd Div
- 3 Brit Inf Div
- 3 Cdn Inf Div
- 43 (W) Inf Div
- 51 (H) Inf Div

Appendix "F"

Itinerary of Main Corps HQ

1944

June	8	Ryes (4 miles N.E. Bayeux)
	13	Nonant (2 miles S.E. Bayeux)
July	28	Trungy (2 miles N. La Belle Epine)
August	4	Quesnay (3 miles N.E. Caumont)
	6	Canteloup (4 miles S.E. Caumont)
	8	Ondefontaine
	17	Proussy (3 miles N.E. Conde)
	18	Taillebois (between Berjou and Briouze)
	19	Le Mesnil (2 miles W. Putanges)
	21	Moulins-sur-Orne (near Argentan)
	23	Orgeres (4 miles S.E. Gace)
	26	Douains (3 miles S.W. Vernon)
	29	Haricourt (3 miles N. Vernon)
	30	Dangu (3 miles S.W. Gisors)
	31	Hebecourt (6 miles S. Amiens)
Sept.	1	Simencourt (7 miles S.W. Arras)
	3	Tournai
	4	Brussels
	7	Diest
	13	Hechtel
	20	Malden (Nijmegen suburb)
	28	Alverna (5 miles W. Nijmegen)
Oct.	9	Wijchen (6 miles W. Nijmegen)
Nov.	9	Beek (near Maastricht)
Dec.	13	Boxtel (12 miles N.W. Eindhoven)
	20	Hasselt

www.ingramcontent.com/pod-product-compliance
Lightning Source LLC
Chambersburg PA
CBHW061542010526
44113CB00023B/2774